Jesús Campos

THE AMERICAIDA

Geopolitical Studies: Neo-Latin Americanism
From Bolívar to Galeano. FINAL CALL

THE AMERICAIDA

jesusmcamposv@gmail.com

@rubianoediciones

First edition: 2024

ISBN: 978-980-18-5411-1

Editorial coordination
Elisabel Rubiano
Graphic design
Carmen Maura Peralta
Proofreading
Álvaro Valderas
Cover and back cover images
Cristóbal Colón llega a América, Theodor de Bry, 1594, Rijksmuseum.
N. Visscher, *Atlas Contractus Orbis Terrarum*, 1659.

"We are all Americans and rightful owners of the land where we were born. Let us ensure that love binds the children of Columbus's hemisphere with a universal bond."

Simón Bolívar

"Unity accomplishes everything, and for this reason, we must preserve this precious principle."

Simón Bolívar

"Let each one do their part of duty, and nothing shall vanquish us."

José Martí

"There are circumstances in life when one must risk everything if one wishes to continue living, both physically and morally."

Benito Juárez

"The history of Latin America is the history of the plunder of natural resources."

Eduardo Galeano

"What I desire for my children, I desire for my people."

Omar Torrijos

"Today's inequality cannot be attributed solely to insatiable capitalist gluttony, although it is indisputable that this was the architect and sustainer of its initial creation and development."

Rubén Blades

PROLOGUE

Some ideas show such a degree of evidence that it seems impossible they haven't materialized yet. One of these is the union of Spanish-American countries and Brazil into a single economic and social bloc. If the European Union is possible, even if only circumstantially, bringing together countries separated by resentment, history, culture, recent or desired economic models, and even language, why wouldn't a new Spanish-Ibero-Latin America be possible?

Its geographical limits are more inclusive than exclusive. It would rightfully include Spanish-speaking countries, Brazil, and French-speaking American countries, with the initial exception of Canada. Dutch-speaking American territories could be incorporated with special status. After this starting point, the relevance of other incorporations would be studied, as well as whether or not to make special agreements with Spain, Portugal, Canada, and France.

Its social and cultural boundaries are much clearer in popular knowledge, regardless of the language spoken in each country. There have been frictions between some, undoubtedly logical in a historical neighborhood with a fire stoked by foreign powers interested in controlling these states as private estates from which to extract benefits and take them to their distant, foreign metropolises.

As a whole, its natural reserves are not only among the largest in the world but also among the most usable, as there is an infrastructure that allows for their exploitation. The resources over which future wars will be unleashed, such as fishing, oil, mining, water, and space, are abundant here. Why does its population have such high poverty rates? The answer is complex: it combines the ruthless and homicidal policy of imperialism—especially American—with its assassination, installation and removal of presidents, its support for terrorism, revolts, and coups, its economic sanctions and purchase of leaders, with a policy aimed at generating poor education and also a widespread permissiveness with inequality and corruption. Even in this chaotic situation, the poorest country in the region has a large number of enormous personal or family fortunes that, if well distributed, would go a long way towards raising the standard of living and eradicating poverty.

This work, like others before it, proposes that union, recovering Bolívar's dream from a current perspective. The most important thing, in the way of doing it, is not exactly what it proposes, as each point can be discussed, nuanced, and changed, but all the topics it covers: economic fusion, yes, but also cultural; geographical fusion, yes, but also military and with a viable defense system against the superpowers that have traditionally intervened in its territory.

It's true that each reader will be more inclined to one economic system than another, but that doesn't prevent this book from serving as a base document for dialogue, which must lead to a *Latin American* union as soon as possible, before the train of history passes by and the greed of the usual suspects, internal and external, makes it unfeasible to improve the living conditions of more than six hundred million people who, together, would be unstoppable.

Álvaro Valderas

INTRODUCTION TO *THE AMERICAIDA*

This title, *The Americaida*, is nothing but an evocation of one of the greatest literary works in history: Homer's *Iliad*. While the *Iliad* is the epic of the battle between Achaeans and Trojans, *The Americaida* aims to represent the struggle of Latin American peoples for their true independence, to be truly independent. This means not being under the protection or domination of any foreign economic, political, or military force, and being culturally sovereign. Not being puppets, satellites, pawns, or the backyard of any foreign power.

If the Ibero-American countries were to unite, in a decade we would cease to be called *third world countries*. We could even become a prosperous and developed region, as long as we renounce savage ideologies like communism (its own theorists argue that there was a primitive communism) and barbaric ones like capitalism (arising with the private ownership of land and production). With capitalism in its barbaric stage came greed, pillage, plunder, and speculation in the exchange of goods. All for the sordid pursuit of profit.

My Vision of Latin America

They call Latin American countries third world, but this is a mistaken perception. For centuries we have had a literary production that has not stopped, Latin America has great writers in each of its countries, poets, playwrights, novelists; we also have great thinkers and philosophers, as well as countless academics and professors who have been educated at the best universities in the world. We have great master painters, sculptors, architects. We can build our own civil works thanks to talented civil engineers. Here we have scientists of the highest caliber, researchers, and developers. In music, needless to say, we have singer-songwriters, performers, composers, arrangers, and singers to go around the world. In sports, there are world-famous legends. What about natural resources, for which the powers have always wanted to exploit and take over the riches.

The severe problem in Latin America is its disproportionate socioeconomic inequality, a product of the model imposed on us by capitalist powers, as this way we will always be under their ideological and hegemonic umbrella. This is also possible thanks to the elitist classes that follow instructions from these powers.

This problem that has not yet been resolved is the cause in Latin America of extreme poverty, slums, violence, crime that leads to organized crime, and, likewise, public and private corruption and large migrations to developed countries in search of better opportunities to live.

THE CONSOLIDATION OF BOLÍVAR'S DREAM

We must develop our own social, legal, political, and economic system that will lead us to the highest civilizational stages never reached by any society. We must move away from systems of corrupt governments, peoples plunged into poverty and ignorance, cartels and guerrillas terrorizing towns and cities. Economic and political power concentrated in a few oligarch-bourgeois families. There is violence and civil disobedience everywhere.

This is what Latin America has had to live since the Spanish colonies and Brazil decided to become independent and become sovereign and independent republics. Since we ceased to be Spanish and Portuguese colonies almost two centuries ago, we have been governed by all kinds of government systems, almost all corrupt, weak democracies where parties of all ideologies parade causing a setback with each change of government and, in the interim, civil wars, military dictatorships, citizen discontent that ends in revolts and street protests that lead to police repression, torture, disappearances. All this has led us to one place: to make Latin American countries third world states governed by a rich oligarch-bourgeois elite at the service of the interests of hegemonic superpowers.

The countries of Ibero-America need a change of course as soon as possible. Their unity will be fundamental to make this great movement. Together we could leap from the third world to become a prosperous and peaceful region. We have natural resources and the strength of our people; we just need to agree and not allow any foreign power to intervene and conspire against our unity. Liberal democracies are only struggles for political and economic power and irreconcilable ideological conflicts.

The present ideal of political improvement is a federative coordination of related sociological groups, which respects their own characteristics and harmonizes them in a powerful common nationality. No historical convergence seems more natural than a federation of the peoples of Latin America. Dispersed a century ago by lack of communication and feudalism, they can now raise again the problem of their future national unity, extended from the Rio Grande to the Strait of Magellan. This historical possibility deserves to become a common ideal, since the hopes of progress and the dangers of vassalage are common to all peoples. It is time to repeat that, if such a destiny were not to be fulfilled, its colonization by the imperialism that has been stalking them for a hundred years would be inevitable: the oblique Monroe Doctrine, firm will of the United States, expresses today its decision to tutor and exploit our Latin America, captivating it without violence through dollar diplomacy. Its accomplices are political tyranny, economic parasitism and religious superstition, which need to keep our peoples divided, exploiting their reciprocal hatreds in favor of the interests created in a hundred years of traditional feudalism.

Faced with these immoral forces of the past, the hope of approaching a firm solidarity can only be placed in the

New Generation. May it be capable of resisting the small temptations of the present, while acquiring the moral forces that enable it to undertake our great work of the future: to develop social justice in the continental nationality.

José Ingenieros: *Las fuerzas morales*

The main objectives of creating UELA are:

- To maintain peace and avoid any military conflict between the countries that form the Union through the Inter-American Court for Conflict Resolution.
- To prevent the imposition of autocratic regimes.
- At the macroeconomic level, to work as a single economic bloc. To unite our economies.
- This economic bloc should transform into progress and wealth for the peoples that make up the Union.
- To create a common Latin American trade that reduces imports and promotes more trade between the countries of the union.
- To avoid at all costs foreign powers meddling in matters concerning UELA and to prevent any international organisation from imposing economic policies to the detriment of UELA member countries.
- The creation of a currency for common use by all UELA member states. (This currency could be printed in both Spanish and Portuguese, and will have the same exchange value in member states). To control inflation and capital flight.

• Creation of the Latin American Trade Committee for good commercial and customs relations in a win-win or mutually beneficial arrangement.

• It would be a supranational body of the countries that comprise it (Union of Latin American States; UELA), with a permanent headquarters in a Latin American country.

• An economic union through monetary equalisation or through the creation of a common currency for all of Latin America. A common currency that consolidates the common economic and financial system, but not based on capitalist or communist models.

• To create the Latin American Development Bank with state funds from members. And to rid ourselves of foreign debts that undermine our economies and burden our peoples. To create a common financial aid fund to avoid further dependence on IFIs.

• To reduce to zero the external debt in all UELA member states.

• To create the Latin American Academy of Sciences and Arts, to encourage research and development of the arts. And with the aim of creating and developing our own scientific, technological and industrial revolution to avoid dependence on foreign industry.

• To consolidate the spirit of the Amphictyonic Congress of 1856.

• To unify the political model, the democratic one, and not tolerate under any circumstances coups d'état or authoritarian regimes. The left and right party-cratic model has already collapsed. We must seek new models of public administration that are more efficient, with high quality standards and highly competitive.

- To protect and conserve our environment.

- To efficiently exploit our natural resources for our own benefit.

- To achieve five Latin American universities ranking among the fifty best in the world.

- To maximise our cultures and values and not be mere consumers of foreign cultures.

- To be able to operate as a bloc before international organisations.

- To smooth over all the historical rough edges that we have been carrying (wars, dictatorships, social and political conflicts). If Europe could create the European Union, why can't we?

- To maintain a dialogue of cordiality and mutual respect with other powers.

- To create the Military Alliance of Latin American States for common defence and to avoid being under threat from any hegemonic power.

- Not to allow any advice on security or defence matters from any government that does not belong to this Latin American Union. To ensure our territory is not leased for military exercises by foreign powers. The UELA Security and Defence Council will be created for this purpose.

- In case of a threat from a foreign power that intends to invade the territory of any or all member countries, to activate the UELA Security and Defence Council.

• To neutralise any attempt at a coup d'état against a member state. And, if necessary, to overthrow it through the activation of the Security and Defence Council.

• The world and the powers will be against this Latin American unity, so they will want to destroy it at the slightest attempt to organise, creating confusion, crisis and instability, something we must not allow.

• Of all the objectives, perhaps the most important will be: to remove Latin American countries from the top positions on lists regarding: illiteracy, unemployment, poverty, malnutrition, delinquency, criminality, organised crime, government corruption and socioeconomic inequality.

• The great challenge and the great victory of Latin Americanism will be to remove all foreign multinationals and replace them with Latin American companies and industries.

• Another great victory will be to impose harsh penalties on corrupt rulers, military personnel and businesspeople.

• We can never allow ourselves to be the backyard and quarry of any foreign power; let us exploit our resources for our own benefit.

Latin America is culturally stagnant in underdevelopment. We must begin by reducing the large number of leisure venues; bars, pubs, nightclubs and dance clubs throughout the region that in many cases generate violence and crime. Reduce alcohol consumption, smoking habits and drug use. Reduce to the maximum degree the habit of watching television and increase the habit of reading, studying, researching, entrepreneurship and other artistic and cultural activities throughout the region.

There are three major obstacles that Latin Americanism must overcome to achieve unity: the economic elites who are at the service of large global capitalist interests, the structure of governmental corruption, and the cartels and criminal gangs. It would be a titanic and marathon task, almost utopian and quixotic, to eliminate them.

Possibly, the three are linked to each other, like three branches of the same trunk.

Why is the cost of living so high in Latin American countries? Why do Latin American countries suffer from inflation and devaluation of their currencies? Why are Latin American countries indebted to international financial organisations? Latin America lives subjected to the international financial-capitalist system, subjected by speculators and by an endless chain of intermediaries to the profit of bank interests and burdensome fiscal taxes.

With a system of collective or corporate bodies, we will all win. In other words, we advocate for an economic system based on cooperativism and corporatism, and redesigning a positivist socio-political model, free from political ideologies and religious doctrines.

WHY THE CREATION OF THE UNION OF LATIN AMERICAN STATES?"

Let's take these examples: United States, United Kingdom, European Union, United Nations, Union of Soviet Socialist Republics (until 1991), United Arab Emirates, and African Union. These states, kingdoms, and organizations decided to unite and become great and important countries capable of decisively influencing history.

Spanish-American peoples and Brazil should have the same vision of seeking their unity, perhaps not in a single state, but in an organization in the form of an alliance that advocates unitedly for their common interests and, why not, become influential on the world stage and, above all, most importantly: become developed nations and not be subjected to or threatened by economic and military powers that have only seen us as a quarry to exploit our natural resources, which are many and abundant.

Due to the historical, social, and cultural ties that unite us, it is now a priority, more than urgent, to create UELA (Union of Latin American States) among all Latin American nations, to chart their own roadmaps through mutual cooperation. This would be a Latin American alliance created and directed by Latin Americans to safeguard their interests.

UELA would be an organization with four axes of action: economic, political, military, cultural, and legal. A Latin

American court to see high-profile crimes of politicians and military personnel and a court of arbitration between Latin American States. Economically, prosperity must be ensured and the development of member countries achieved so that they are, once and for all, a preponderant piece on the game board of nations.

Regarding international organizations where several Latin American countries are subscribed, there may be a single representation under the figure of UELA representative before that organization.

Latin American countries have been unfortunate from their beginnings. First, the exploitative domination of the Spanish Empire, then they have been subjected to brutal dictatorial regimes, often in collusion and with the blessing of foreign powers to negotiate with a corrupt tyrant the great natural resources these countries possess. And they have suffered disastrous fratricidal civil wars, equally plotted by foreign powers. It is the supreme priority of UELA to prevent any usurpation of political power and mitigate any attempt at a coup d'état, and to avoid at all costs that a Latin American country falls under undemocratic principles. It will be the supreme power of UELA to intervene militarily in any country suffering these threats and to reimpose democratic constitutional order. This will be possible thanks to a treaty of democratic intervention signed by all Latin American countries.

The Union of Latin American States can be conceived through a referendum in each invited country or through a congress where the president of each invited country decides to be part of UELA.

As a first step, to approve or disapprove through a referendum being a member state of UELA. In case a country approves its integration into UELA, the dignitaries of said country will formalize their participation through an Amphictyonic Congress by signing the charter.

The Four Pillars of UELA

- **Economic and financial unity.** aims to turn us into an economic power. Create our own economic model, a new economic model far from the inequalities produced by capitalism and the poverty produced by communism.
- **Political homogeneity.** Try to make all member countries democratic, but not under the collapsed party-cratic model dominated by right or left ideologies.
- **Military unity or coalition.** Safeguard unity from any foreign threat but without pretension of being a military power or threat to other states.
- **Create a Latin American Academy of Sciences and Arts.** Enhance and make important contributions to sciences, raise education to the highest standards and put Latin American culture above other cultures.
- **Legal.** Create courts of conciliation, mediation, and arbitration where member states can resolve conflicts in the first instance.

Countries Invited to be Part of this Great Union of Latin American States

México Venezuela Brasil
Guatemala Ecuador Uruguay
Honduras Perú Paraguay
Nicaragua Bolivia Rep. Dominicana
El Salvador Chile Cuba
Costa Rica Argentina
Puerto Rico (como Estado soberano)
Panamá Colombia

Second Great Amphictyonic Congress of Latin American Countries

The idea is to convene an assembly of all Latin American countries including Brazil, Cuba, and Puerto Rico to discuss matters of general interest in the region. Countries in the region such as Haiti, Belize, Suriname, Jamaica, and Trinidad and Tobago may be invited.

In this amphictyonic congress, the constitutive principles of what will be the Union of Latin American States (UELA) should be outlined along with the coalition or military alliance of Latin American States (UELA Security and Defense Council).

Among the main points to be discussed would be imperative issues for total and absolute independence and sovereignty of UELA:

1. Declare that the era of expansionism and interference in Latin American affairs has ended for hegemonic states.

2. All of Latin America will be free from Freemasonry and its false libertarian and democratic ideals.

3. Free from foreign religions, brought by colonizers to impose their creeds.

4. The elimination of Non-Governmental Organizations (NGOs) or International Cooperation Agencies (ICAs), which are financed by foreign lobbies, often to do sustainable soft espionage work and thus influence economic, social, cultural, political, legal, and even moral aspects.

5. Free from foreign transnational companies and start developing our own industries.

6. Renounce any cooperation agreement on security and defense with hegemonic states.

7. Trade and neutrality treaties will be negotiated with hegemonic states.

8. Latin American finances will be de-dollarized.

9. A common currency will be created for UELA.

10. We will work in favor of our Latin American culture and identity and avoid all foreign cultural influence: cinema, music, television programs.

11. UELA will be the first and only instance to resolve internal conflicts of each member state and conflicts between member states, both those internal of economic, political and social orders and conflicts between member states of legal or warlike order.

Our greatest goal is actually the fervent and necessary desire to escape from all shadow of the umbrella of influence by hegemonic states that has lasted for the last two hundred years and achieve independence; economic, political and cultural.

HISTORY OF LATIN AMERICAN COUNTRIES

Spanish America and Brazil

While it is true that Spanish America and Brazil have different origins, and that we are separated by history and language, it is also very true that our origins are parallel and occur in the same circumstances and era. During the conquests carried out by Spain and Portugal in the New World in the 16th century, the same sociological, cultural, political and economic phenomena occurred.

Our conquerors, Spain and Portugal, have a similar history, as they were once a single territory and a single kingdom. During their conquests in America, both were considered naval and mercantile powers; their colonies were not only in America, but also in Africa and Asia. Their ships ploughed almost all the oceans and seas.

Therefore, an integration of Ibero-American countries with the great Brazil would be almost as natural due to the ties that unite us. And, above all, it would be an unprecedented geopolitical and socioeconomic strategy in the history of our nations. It would be a mutually beneficial integration, a firm step towards achieving total independence from hegemonic powers in Latin American affairs. It will be necessary to use a tool such as diplomacy. UELA could have the right to represent all member states before international organisations and to make trade treaties as a bloc with other countries or with large economic groups.

To give authentic democratic validity to Latin American integration, UELA must be legitimised by the will of the citizens through a referendum in each country that wishes to be a member, so that UELA is not an organisation imposed and orchestrated behind the backs of the peoples that would form it, as they should ultimately be the main beneficiaries.

Spanish American Countries and Brazil Free Themselves from the Yoke of their European Conquerors

The nations of Spanish America gained independence from the Kingdom of Spain thanks to English support in weaponry, ammunition and soldiers, and above all, financial aid. By then, Spain had ceased to be an empire and had become a weakened kingdom, as it was under the dominion of French troops, who were attempting to impose a republic under Napoleon as emperor. English mining companies exchanged the coal found only on their island for the gold, silver, copper and iron that abound in South American territories, with cheap labour and almost all the profits for themselves. These enormous riches, instead of going to Spain, would change course to the British Empire, thus delivering one of the most humiliating slaps in commercial and geopolitical history.

Revisionist history suggests that the British Empire may have been the architect of the War of the Triple Alliance against Paraguay and of provoking the genocide against the Paraguayan people.

From the second half of the 20th century to date, regional integration initiatives and organisations conceived outside the OAS have been more numerous than is usually remembered. These organisations have emerged at different times, for various reasons and in the context of different projects, according to their respective circumstances. Some were created in the heat of the democratic-popular and anti-colonialist moment that followed World War II, others with the impetus of ECLAC development (ECLAC), or the rise of Latin American nationalism, etc. As a result, today each one acts in the field of its respective functions, with insufficient overall vision to articulate as parts of a common project or a regional body to coordinate them.

Nils Castro. Latin America and the Caribbean: Emancipatory or Neocolonial Integration.

The British Empire and its Influence in Latin America

There has not been a corner on Earth where the British have not attempted to impose their quota of power or influence, whether through invasion, occupation or conquest.

The British Empire was not created thanks to a planned or future vision, but rather was a desperate action to emulate the conquests carried out by the Spanish and Portuguese who had found new maritime routes to trade with the East. With these two words: “envy” and “greed”.

With the Spanish and Portuguese conquests in new lands in America and Africa, colonialism and domination of new lands, Spain became the first great modern overseas empire and Portugal the first modern maritime power. The English crown would not allow it for long, as it considered that the great historical privilege of being the great conquerors of the new lands had been usurped from them and because they considered the Spanish and Portuguese inferior: the great conspiracy with English piracy was conceived to sow terror and truncate Spanish trade not only by sea, but they also invaded and destroyed Spanish cities in America as a consequence of these incursions by English mercenaries, who, by order of the crown, managed to bring down the Spanish empire and conquer the Portuguese routes through Africa and reach India. So that it would never recover again. After this, the English, now with their own Navy, began to make incursions into Spanish cities and ports in America. They created an advanced espionage agency, a legion of conspirators and a network of smuggler merchants to have commercial and political control over Spanish American territories.

The English set out to conquer any overseas territory not conquered by Europeans and establish colonies there, whether by enslaving, exploiting, expropriating, usurping and even massacring villagers if necessary to dominate their new territories and thus forge the vast British Empire.

English piracy wreaked havoc in the Caribbean, looting and ravaging the first Spanish colonies in America. The results were catastrophic for the Spanish crown and the great empire saw how it was crumbling. All thanks to the pillage promoted, tutored and orchestrated with great approval by the English crown: the action of pirates, privateers and filibusters, mercenaries; cruel, ruthless, bloodthirsty and lawless.

British Freemasonry and its Influence in Latin America

Freemasonry is the ideology of the oligarch-bourgeois of Latin America. It has its origins in the British Empire from the 18th century, around the year 1717, created by Protestants. They want to give it medieval and chivalrous origins, but there is no historical or archaeological evidence. Our most illustrious founding fathers naively fell for this ideology and drank the masonic hemlock. They were seduced by its false ideals of liberty, equality and fraternity. But, especially, they sought British support in the struggle for independence of Latin American nations from the Spanish yoke.

Freemasonry is today the ideal way for the British Empire to have access to economic, social and political powers in Latin America.

Once Freemasonry infiltrated the oligarchy and the bourgeoisie, these would be more manipulable. But now the poor and ignorant masses were missing, who were eminently Catholic, contrary to Masonic foundations. This work would fall to the United States, an unconditional ally of the British Empire. In the mid-20th century, waves of preachers from all Protestant sects began to arrive in Latin America in order to found these sects and establish Protestant sects throughout Latin American countries and diminish the doctrinal power of the Catholic Church, taking away parishioners and converting them into new Protestants and enemies of Catholicism. Today they are called "evangelicals", and belong to the most varied North American Protestant sects: Adventists, Methodists, Baptists, Episcopalians and Pentecostals, along with Jehovah's Witnesses and Mormons. These sects currently span from Mexico to Argentina and Brazil, even reaching indigenous tribes. They all have connections and are controlled from the United States. Today, in Latin America these sects have millionaire resources and millions of adherents.

The de facto powers are dominated by Freemasonry and the dominated masses by Protestant sects. The New Latin America must free itself from these foreign ideologies that oppress us. Latin America will have a great task in getting rid of so much Anglo-Saxon influence that subjugates us.

The first thing to do is to suppress all foreign fanaticism and light the torch of science, reason and knowledge.

G. W. F. Hegel comments on Freemasonry in *Introduction to the History of Philosophy* as follows:

One could suspect in Freemasonry a similar purpose in its symbols and myths; but no injustice will be done to it when one is convinced that there is no special knowledge there; consequently, it also has nothing to hide. But that it is not in possession nor has in custody any wisdom, science or special knowledge, nor is it in possession of any truth...

Therefore, Freemasonry is neither religion, nor philosophy, nor science, nor art; thus, perhaps it is an esoteric-occultist sect, but endorsed by the Anglican Church.

Anglo-hegemonism, Anglo-centrism and Anglo-supremacism

Every ideology needs its propaganda apparatus to consolidate its power to influence. This apparatus is its best tool for disseminating and spreading its ideals.

This powerful mechanism of mass manipulation has perhaps the most powerful propaganda machinery in history: the Hollywood film and entertainment industry. This large media industry produces films almost like hot cakes, and these films reach all corners of the planet.

There is nothing more similar to Plato's cave myth than cinema. Almost all films are written, produced and directed by Americans or British, for obvious reasons. Thanks to a global chain of cinemas and without any kind of censorship regarding the morals of other cultures, through brainwashing, they impose their culture, language and idiosyncrasy; or that we think as they wish within a type of mass indoctrination. We worship and idolise their actors and singers, who act as superheroes with superhuman powers or daring policemen who save the world. They are presented to us as attractive, powerful, astute and invincible. They also like to display in their films all their military, technological and economic power, to impose their supremacist ideology.

In most action films, Hollywood tries to create invincible heroes who, with their cunning and sagacity, save humanity from all kinds of threats, making the social psyche think that the United States or the United Kingdom are the world's safeguards. In the films, these heroes are always presented as the good guys and as the smartest, being able to overcome all dangers and threats with the necessary cunning to end and destroy their enemies, who are always the bad guys, the greatest threat to the world. To fulfil their mission, these super agents leave behind a flood of homicides and destruction that remain in total impunity, although in reality this is a product of Hollywood magic.

The United States and the United Kingdom are great military, political and economic allies, as both have had many common interests for more than two centuries.

The intelligence services of the United States are at the service of the United Kingdom, and vice versa. They also maintain an exchange of military equipment and technology between them.

And, between both countries, they have decided to impose their political, economic and military hegemony, committing innumerable crimes against humanity that have remained in the most ignominious impunity.

British-American Hegemony and its Capitalist Power: Military-Industrial-Usurious

From the Industrial Revolution, largely thanks to the transfer of technology from India and China once subjugated as colonies by the British Empire, and with the emergence of capitalism as an economic doctrine during the first half of the 18th century, the English believed themselves to be the nation par excellence, destined to dominate the world. They initiated a colonialist and domination campaign on a global scale, reaching all corners of the world to tell them that they were their new lords. They freely dedicated themselves to enslaving peoples considered culturally inferior, according to the British canon. Any people or state that opposed their colonialist and mercantilist interests was brutally subjugated by their military force, always with the support of mercenary armies that guaranteed their victory. Between the 18th and 20th centuries, the British Empire has been involved in almost all military conflagrations, using the technological advances of the Industrial Revolution in the service of war, obtaining important victories, so much so that it was considered an invincible empire. From these victories, their main purpose was to gain mercantile, geopolitical and diplomatic advantages; they made English the international language for commerce and therefore considered themselves the most important and rich citizens of the world.

While the British Empire consolidated its power and influence on a global level, its former colony in America, the United States, was tenaciously preparing to follow in its footsteps and continue the legacy of imposing Western capitalist culture worldwide. In the second half of the 20th century, after World War II, the United States consolidated itself as the first economic, military and political power. Since then, it has dedicated itself to pursuing its own agenda of war and domination, in which organisations such as the UN are incapable of containing its power. Like their British mentors, the United States has dedicated itself to creating tensions in countries that are far from its borders. We are always on edge about a Third World War due to the unilateral and supremacist decisions of the United States. There is a great possibility that a nuclear Armageddon will be unleashed due to the constant supremacist humiliations over other peoples and cultures.

WORLD PEACE AND ITS BRITISH-AMERICAN INFLUENCE

The World Bank and the International Monetary Fund

Both the World Bank and the International Monetary Fund have their headquarters in Washington. They were born from the Bretton Woods agreements in 1944. During the negotiations, it was established how the new world financial order would be shaped. How can two banks of such magnitude be created simultaneously? Possibly, funds were transferred from the United States Federal Reserve to create them. The dollar was established as the official currency for international finance, thus allowing them to move their funds without restrictions worldwide. From then until now, the World Bank and the International Monetary Fund have been controlled by the financial elites of both the United States and the United Kingdom.

With the financial power of the United States Federal Reserve, they threaten all states to provide their natural resources and thus move their industries and businesses.

They have subjected developing countries to an unpayable and burdensome external debt: supreme capitalism in its maximum expression.

In Washington D.C., two governments function: one that oversees internal affairs—managing internal security, as in any other country in the world—and another that aims to govern the world, claiming that everything that happens outside its territory can affect its hegemonic, political, military, commercial, and financial interests. But, on the other side of the Atlantic, many beans are still being cooked in the City of London in economic and financial matters.

For this, they spread all kinds of cooperation agencies or NGOs around the world as diplomatic and intelligence arms.

The UN

The United Nations Organisation, UN, despite having been created after the Second World War as an international body to prevent military conflicts and help alleviate the global problems that humanity had already been suffering. From that very moment, the United States considered itself to have the supreme right to intervene in any conflict in the world, and it became the great world gendarme, with the ability to move across its grand geopolitical chessboard where it would have the capacity to move all its pieces.

NATO

Parallel to the creation of the UN, the North Atlantic Treaty Organisation was created. Why is it called North Atlantic? Because the North Atlantic is the area of the Atlantic Ocean that strategically unites the United States and the United Kingdom, and which is under their control and dominion. It is a military alliance whose absolute control is under these two states in order to maintain and deploy their hegemony throughout the world and keep their military industries alive to leave them high profitability.

They not only want to control and dominate the North Atlantic; their intention is to control all the seas and oceans of the world through their expansion with the adhesion of new satellite allies in Europe and with an unprecedented deployment of military bases around the world, apparently in perpetuity.

NATO is simply the letter of marque with which the United States and the United Kingdom claim their right to the spoils of war from World War II, which is Europe, and goes in pursuit of conquering Eastern Europe and, at the same time, provoking Russia and China with military manoeuvres near their territories, but these two superpowers know how to defend themselves and how to attack.

The other NATO allies are merely satellite partners who must submissively cede part of their territory and sovereignty to install military bases under British and American control and thus freely use their territories, territorial seas and territorial spaces for the implementation of military exercises without any specific or concrete reason.

The majority of NATO's satellite allied countries are pacifist nations that avoid conflict among their European brothers, but due to their geographical positions, they are useful to the hegemonic interests of their two main partners. These countries cannot renounce NATO because they would receive harsh sanctions and reprisals.

Why, in a unified Europe such as the European Union is now and in full peace, do American and British military bases still exist that violate sovereignties as if these European countries were protectorates under their power or as if we were on the brink of a great military conflagration?

It is regrettable that these countries, considered first powers of the Western world, suffer from war paranoia. Their current rulers speak in their speeches on foreign policy about their enemies and allies. They speak little of peace and prosperity for all peoples.

For peace or world stability to exist, the United States and the United Kingdom cannot continue to consider themselves international gendarmes and judges in all conflicts just for having won World War II, under the pretext of safeguarding their hegemonic interests.

For stability to begin in the world, nations that have American and British military bases should demand that they vacate their territory, as they violate their sovereignty. In Panama, the almost century-old American military bastion was brought to an end, although it had to be paid for with the death of a significant number of citizens and a military invasion called “Just Cause”.

There will be no peace or world stability as long as the United States and the United Kingdom maintain a military presence outside their borders and spy agents throughout the world. Undoubtedly, they have every right to defend their interests, but they should do so within their borders and under the framework of mutual respect and international law. This would be a first great step towards geopolitical stability.

For true and lasting peace to exist in the world, the United States and the United Kingdom must withdraw all their military bases stationed outside their borders so that their destroyers, aircraft carriers and submarines only navigate within their coasts or territorial seas, and their satellites and telecommunications equipment cease spying on the world.

When this happens, they will realise that their enemies have only been windmills, that no country in the world wishes to wage war with the United States or the United Kingdom; they take as an enemy anyone who does not bow or submit to their will, any state that does not allow its resources to be exploited in exchange for crumbs.

Let the UN and other international organisations solve conflicts through negotiating tables. Dismantling NATO would be another great step, as vast financial resources are allocated just to play at war and provocation, which could trigger a military conflict of apocalyptic proportions. Another great step towards peace would be to dismantle all nuclear weapons and use atomic technology only for uses that benefit humanity. And these objectives can very well be carried out by the UN.

The United States and its Military Actions During the 20th and 21st Centuries

The United States has participated in almost all military conflicts of the 20th century and what has elapsed of the 21st century. At the end of the 19th century, they decided—without apparent reason—to declare war on Spain to seize

Florida, Cuba, Puerto Rico and the Philippines, and thus take control over the Gulf of Mexico and the Caribbean Sea, and have a bastion in the distant Pacific; it was the first great American military colonialism of the late 19th century. They initiated the war with Mexico to take possession of California and Texas and achieve a great extension on the Pacific West Coast. They participated in World War I, an eminently European war carried out due to properly European conflicts. They participated in World War II, provoked by purely European reasons, in which their ally, the United Kingdom, was involved, so they took part to take some of the spoils.

The United States had the fortune that despite having participated in the two great world wars, its territory was never a battlefield. It was undoubtedly the great victor of the world wars.

In the midst of World War II, at the naval base of Pearl Harbor, the United States stationed warships almost ready to enter the military conflict, capable of almost dominating the entire Pacific. But it was nothing more than a lure to provoke an attack by the Japanese, as if they had placed a garden with fragrant flowers to attract bees and delight in their nectar. The thousands of dead and mutilated sailors were a great quota of sacrifice and heroism.

This was the great bait to justify the entry of the United States into World War II and thus support its eternal ally, the British Empire. Once the United States decided to enter the Second War almost overnight—or perhaps this was prepared long before—to set in motion a colossal arms industry, the largest and unprecedented in history, and this great war industry has not stopped since then.

They recruited hundreds of thousands of their young people from the countryside and towns, but not the young people from banking and the stock market.

They built bomber planes to annihilate almost all of Europe. Many of these air bombardments fell on churches, hospitals, schools, universities, houses, apartments, museums, libraries, historical monuments in numerous European towns; even sacred Rome itself was a victim of these unpunished and inhuman bombardments by the Allies in World War II.

The United States devises and develops the atomic bomb, which can be considered the most macabre plan carried out by a civilised country in the history of humanity. They dropped two atomic bombs on two defenceless Japanese cities that posed no potential threat. This has made the United States the only and greatest atomic genocidaire in history, although, due to its great power, this genocide will go unpunished. And this weapon will also serve to open the doors to a Third Atomic World War, in which there will be no winner and the Earth will reach its maximum destruction and the total annihilation of life.

In World War II, they seduced the Japanese, who in reality were a small empire compared to the military superpower of the USA, and in this way they waged a war at their leisure in the Pacific to gain full control of the world's largest ocean. Then, they decided that Japan would be the fertile ground to test atomic bombs, perhaps considering the Japanese racially and culturally inferior.

Once positioned as a world power, the USA imposed its economic and political model on the world, but its former ally, the USSR, with its communist and tyrannical ideology, took control of Eastern Europe and communist China began its race to also become a world power.

With these great obstacles against them, the Cold War begins between the USA and the USSR, both with their great allies: the United Kingdom for the USA and China for the Soviets. From these same conflicts arises the Korean War, and the United States decides to be guardians of democratic and liberal values. Communist China takes Vietnam and the USA again assumes the role of world gendarme and participates in a military conflict where they had nothing to gain, only to demonstrate their immense military capacity, which, in the end, turned out to be their most humiliating defeat of the 20th century.

In the 20th century, the USA has participated directly or indirectly in every military conflict, whether in selling weapons to their allies, or even to their opponents.

Towards the end of the 20th century, Iraq, their former military client, decided to invade Kuwait and the USA arrogated to itself the right to defend Kuwait as an oil colony and deployed "Desert Storm", the largest military conflict for control of oil in the Middle East, where the United Kingdom also intervenes as a guest, in its capacity as an ally.

They take part in the Balkan war, triggered by ancient ethnic, religious and territorial tensions. There they send planes to bomb any desirable target.

Already in the 21st century, the greatest attack within US territory occurs, 9/11, in New York, and Armageddon trumpets begin to sound and the world fills with anguish and uncertainty, although, due to the way the WTC towers fell, it is suspected that it could have been a self-attack (there is much research on conspiracy theories about this).

Due to these attacks, the USA once again launches into the war adventure and finishes off its former ally and military client Iraq, provoking one of the largest attacks after World War II. Iraq is turned to rubble, destroying any archaeological vestiges of the Assyrian, Sumerian and Babylonian civilisations. And they take advantage of their trip to the Middle East to invade Afghanistan, a country suffering and worn out by invaders seeking to control its oil, and a stronghold of the Taliban, a fundamentalist and extremist group allied with Al Qaeda that harshly oppresses the Afghan people.

The USA has never been a battlefield of any war or military conflict from an external power, which is ironic for a country that has participated in all modern wars. It is better to dedicate oneself to sending troops and armament as far as possible from their borders and that death and destruction do not occur within their home. And they accompany it with the paradoxical premise "We come to bring freedom and democracy".

The bombing of North Korea in 1950, where cities were destroyed and hundreds of thousands of innocent civilians died, is one of many cowardly attacks by the United States when they already see themselves defeated and simply do not accept defeat.

They did the same with the bombings of German cities such as Dresden or Berlin in World War II, and the atomic bombing of Hiroshima and Nagasaki in Japan in the same war, and then the incendiary bombings of Vietnamese villages during the invasion of Vietnam, where only the defenceless and unarmed civilian population was decimated.

The two Koreas will never unify as long as there are American military bases in South Korea. Ireland will never unify as long as the United Kingdom holds its northern part hostage.

The United States is the country that most violates the sovereignty of other countries, humiliating them by imposing military bases in all parts of the world with the excuse that they safeguard the interests of democracy and freedom.

The United States is like this Quixote who sees windmills as monsters; its war psychosis is pathetic.

The United States is too powerful a country to have enemies. It is true that there are groups that hate them, but these groups hate everyone. No country would wish to declare war on the United States, unless it is a country governed by some madman.

The United States seeks enemies even on the internet; it needs to show the world that it is the most powerful and invincible country, a lesson well learned from the Nazis. Before the end of the 20th century, the United States continued with its addiction to bombing towns and cities, and in 1999, they, with their NATO allies, the military arm of the UN, bombed Kosovo in the former Yugoslavia.

Since World War II, it is the only country that has carried out military interventions bypassing the UN Security Council. It has had the world as its stage for harassment, war and espionage.

At the beginning of the 21st century, the ill-fated 9/11 occurs and the United States needed someone to pay for the broken dishes. The unfortunate winner was Iraq, and in 2003 they did what they like best: bomb and destroy cultures. To date, Iraq remains occupied and destroyed, Iraq, the country that housed the ancient civilisations of Sumeria, Akkad, Chaldea, Babylon and Amorrhea.

There is only one path to peace. The United States along with Great Britain must withdraw their military bases that are outside their borders. Especially those disguised as NATO and Blue Helmets, but with full American and British control.

We are still living in post-war times. In 1989 the Berlin Wall fell and with it the post-war and Cold War ended, but there are still American military bases in Germany and many others in European countries.

Both the United States and the United Kingdom have military bases scattered throughout Europe, humiliating countries that have contributed so much to Western culture such as Spain, Portugal, France, Italy and Germany with the sole objective of reminding them who are the masters of the world, as there is no military conflict in Europe since the UN and the EU were created. These military bases are only there to goad the great Russian nation and provoke a third and definitive world war, which would be nuclear.

The EU should make a firm decision and not negotiate diplomatically, but give a firm order for foreign military bases to leave *ipso facto* from its sovereign territory.

This policy of the United States and Great Britain of installing military bases in foreign countries is an imperial policy, in the best style of the Roman Empire. With these militaristic policies, we have regressed almost 2000 years in international law.

But for the Americans and British, the post-war and Cold War have not yet ended.

Let Us Make the World in Our Image and Likeness: An X-ray of the 20th Century

The 20th century would become one of the most brutal in history. Two world wars, the dropping of two atomic bombs, a Cold War that divided the world into two sides with threats of a nuclear holocaust, genocides driven by religious and racial hatred (the Congo; the KKK; Paraguay; Cambodia; Armenia; German Jews; Christians in Africa, the Middle East and Asia; pogroms in Russia, China, Rwanda). We can add the racial segregation regimes of *apartheid* in South Africa, Namibia and Rhodesia; a disastrous Spanish civil war; in Latin America, weak democracies, corrupt and puppet governments, coups d'état, military dictatorships, civil wars, disappeared persons and mass graves; the United States generating military conflicts across the globe: Vietnam, Korea, Grenada, Panama, Iraq, Yugoslavia; the most brutal dictatorships: Spain, Germany,

Italy, Uganda, China, Cuba, USSR, Romania, Burma, Cambodia, Philippines, Singapore.

In the Nuremberg trials of 1945, Nazi leaders were tried and convicted for war crimes, but war crimes by the Allies would not be tried or condemned, crimes against humanity that have remained in the most ignominious impunity.

The United Nations Organisation (UN) was created in 1945, headquartered in New York, to guarantee peace between nations and the defence of human and civil rights. The North Atlantic Treaty Organisation (NATO) was created in Washington D.C. in 1949 to guarantee the American and British military presence in Europe, in a territory they consider under their control, and thus maintain their geopolitical hegemony in the region, neutralising any attempt at a threat from any Eastern European country and Russia.

The 20th century saw the growth of the largest criminal organisations in the history of humanity: liquor smuggling, drug trafficking, arms trafficking, prostitution and international white slave trade, the birth of the pornographic industry, and all these activities with their consequent chains of atrocious murders where the most dangerous and ruthless gangsters, drug lords, mafiosi and hit men became famous and part of the culture. There were wars in the Middle East. In the 20th century, famines occurred in Africa, Asia, the Middle East and Latin America as during no other century. Global warming begins due to deforestation and pollution.

The youth of the second half of the 20th century begins to consume psychotropic drugs and alcohol, to relax their sexual behaviour and to rebel against authorities and public order. All this is thanks in part to the new entertainment industry, cinema and music. Beautiful and dazzling actresses and handsome and seductive singers become the idols of youth, who imitate their attitudes in films and repeat the lyrics of their songs.

The World Bank and the IMF are created in the Bretton Woods agreements. These financial organisations will create unpayable external debt for developing countries, imposing neoliberal economic policies on them.

At the end of the century, the HIV virus was born, which so far has found no cure.

Young people became unrestrained with the unlimited consumption of alcohol and drugs in endless parties.

In reality, this X-ray of the 20th century is an apology against religions. Listening to a priest of any religion saying that God was in our midst in the 20th century would be taken as an act of charlatanism. And, at the same time, against the two countries that have controlled and directed step by step the past century: the United States and the United Kingdom. We are still in time for another country or countries to take the leadership of the world and lead us along new paths.

THE EUROPEAN UNION

The European Union must now fight to be independent of British and American influence, and even more so now that the United Kingdom has voluntarily decided to leave European unity with the so-called Brexit. Perhaps due to its ideology of self-sufficiency and supremacy. However, it remains part of NATO which, apparently, has greater interests than being part of the EU.

A worthy aspirant to occupy the position left by the United Kingdom would be the Russian Federation, as it possesses the cultural, historical and geographical right for its reception in the EU, this would bring great stability and prosperity to Europe.

If the Russian Federation manages to be accepted as a member of the EU, the EU could become the world's leading economy.

With the United Kingdom now out of it, English should not be considered one of the official languages of the organisation, but only the languages of the member countries that make up the EU.

All EU member states that are also satellite partners of NATO should renounce NATO and consolidate and safeguard the real interests of the EU.

The tasks of the 21st century for world peace

Dismantle the obsolete military apparatus such as NATO, created to initiate the post-war period and the Cold War against the USSR and communism. Since its foundation, its only objectives have been:

a. Maintain a permanent military presence by the United States and United Kingdom over Europe and thus prevent it from being self-sufficient.

b. Provocation.

c. Threat.

d. ts expansion towards Eastern Europe, dismantle the Soviet Union and now subjugate the Russian Federation under its control.

NATO does not represent the interests of Europe or the European Union, but the exclusive interests of the United States and the United Kingdom.

Dismantle all American, British and NATO military bases outside their sovereign territories, approximately 400 bases around the world. Withdrawing military bases in Europe would be urgent and vital, as these bases create conflicts of interest with the European Union. Neither the United States nor the United Kingdom belong to the EU. The European Union should create its own security and defence alliance, as it is fully self-sufficient.

Military colonialism is immoral and illegal; this imperialist imposition must be ended as soon as possible.

It is a flagrant violation of the sovereignty of States and International Law.

Russia should be accepted as a member of the European Union, this will bring great stability and prosperity to Europe. This new member (the Russian Federation) could turn the European Union into the most extensive and prosperous economic zone in the world.

In the Middle East, Palestine (recognised as a State), Israel, Lebanon and Syria (rebuilt) should form an economic, commercial and touristic community based on mutual respect and tolerance. And turn that Mediterranean region into one of the best in the world for tourism and trade.

China, India, Pakistan, Korea (reunified), Taiwan (sovereign state), Japan (demilitarised), Philippines, Vietnam, Thailand, Indonesia, Malaysia should form an Asia-Pacific Cooperation Alliance. And avoid being in any external sphere of power.

Nuclear powers should manage to sign a great treaty for nuclear disarmament and use atomic energy for peaceful purposes and in the safest possible way for the environment.

Create a new UN, but among all countries considered third world, and stop seeming as if we lived on different planets.

Its main objectives would be to emerge together from economic misery, fight against the corruption of these countries' rulers and eliminate the violence that suffocates us. And, at the same time, raise education. Eliminate from the new organisation any lobby that influences UN decisions.

States such as Palestine, Taiwan, Tibet and others would be recognised. They will be member countries and would establish diplomatic relations among the other member countries.

It would have five headquarters: one in Central America, South America and the Caribbean; one in Africa; one in the Middle East; one in Asia and another in Oceania. And the General Assemblies could be held at any headquarters.

But it will have a Secretary-General and five Under-Secretaries for each headquarters.

The most important function is to trade among member countries and not to trade with economic powers. To be fully sovereign, so that no power imposes trade or exploitation of their natural resources. And maintain good relations of respect and harmony.

Once the organisation is consolidated, countries belonging to the UN may cease to be signatory members and remain as observers.

The first important issues to be addressed by the new UN would be:

- Refugees.
- Human trafficking.
- Slavery.
- Child labour.
- Sexual exploitation.
- Stateless persons.
- Famine.

- Environmental conservation.
- Negotiate with terrorists and seek peaceful solutions.
- Human rights.
- Interfaith tolerance and respect.
- Fight against poverty and inequality.
- Preschool and school education.
- Globalisation and world government.
- Peace in all regions of the world.

For each member country, there will be two representatives. A man and a woman. And their votes will be independent.

The UN as an international organisation has failed in its objectives. It has allowed all military operations and armed conflicts of hegemonic countries. It has indolently allowed the interference of the United States and the United Kingdom in the internal affairs of other countries in all latitudes.

The end of imperialism for over 5,000 years. The United States, the British Empire, Russia and China should create working groups to eliminate their military hegemonies on the planet. Not create wars or military conflicts where millions of people are affected and suffer the ravages due to unscrupulous corporations thirsty for unlimited power and wealth.

Imperialism throughout its history has killed billions of people, innocent victims. This must be stopped as soon as possible[1].

---

1. Karl Marx said that history was the history of class struggle; I say that history is the history of the struggle for the succession of empires.

The new human rights

1. Respect for oneself.
2. Respect for others.
3. Mutual respect.

THE GENESIS OF THIS PROJECT CALLED UNION OF LATIN AMERICAN STATES (UELA)

Brief history of the Panama Congress of 1826. Results and consequences

Below, I will transcribe Chapter 21 of the book "History of Panama" by the philosopher and historian Moisés Chong.

Since there is little that could be added in terms of historiography, undoubtedly, these quotes below are a source of inspiration and essential material for this work.

The idea of convening a great Amphictyonic Congress in Panama was not favourably received in Washington's political circles. The United States Congress itself decided that the country should not stand in solidarity with the South American nations or sign any pact to prevent interventions by European powers to recover lost territories, while preserving, of course, its freedom to act or decide later as dictated by its interests. On this matter, some national authors have written, such as Dr Octavio Méndez Pereira, Ricardo J. Alfaro, Harmodio Arias Madrid, Justo Arosemena, and personalities from other countries such as Daniel Florencio O'Leary, Alberto Llegas Camargo, Vicente Lecuna, Antonio de la Peña y Reyes, André Marius, Víctor Andrés Belaúnde, etc. There are also publications, studies, agendas, such as Publications of the Carnegie Endowment for International Peace from the Mexican Ministry of Foreign Affairs, "The Constitutive Pact of the Pan-American System"; from the Pan-American Union, a Codification of International Law, dated 1926, Washington.

Let us make some clarifications about the Panama Congress of 1826, which began on 22 June and closed on 15 July of the same year. We must take into account that this Congress was held about three years after the formulation of the Monroe Doctrine, and it came to be a kind of replica or response to the intentions of the North American President, James Monroe, who had made declarations of firm adherence to non-extracontinental intervention in America by nations that formed the Holy Alliance, such as Russia, Spain, etc., reserving for the United States the right to defend Latin America against possible foreign aggressions, particularly Spain, which had clear intentions of recovering what was lost in the continental area of America, although everyone - including the Spaniards themselves - was aware that the Hispanic nation was practically bankrupt and unable to carry out its purposes of territorial and political reconquest. There were antecedents that preluded the Panama meeting of '26, such as the Public Treaty signed in Chile and the United Provinces of the Río de la Plata to aid the Peruvians; another, such as the one agreed upon by Peru with Colombia, and the latter with Mexico for similar purposes. The Jamaica Letter of 6 November 1815 also contains amphictyonic ideals: "The States of the Isthmus of Panama to Guatemala will perhaps form a union. That magnificent portion of America, situated between the two oceans, will in due time be the emporium of the Universe". Not only Bolívar had these flashes, but also the South Americans San Martín, O'Higgins, Mariano Moreno, and the Central American hero, José Cecilio del Valle, and in particular, the Venezuelan precursor of Independence, Francisco de Miranda. Thus, the Panama Congress, as an idea, was not the product of improvisation but the result of solid antecedents that obliged the countries of the Gran Colombian mosaic to act as demanded, not so much by high or elevated ideals, but by circumstances that involved the very security, subsistence and autonomy of these nations recently emerged from Hispanic tutelage.

The Bolivarian doctrine that led its spiritual mentor to propose and carry out the Panama Congress of 1826 was based on the idea of forming a community of "the republics that were formerly Spanish colonies", thus trying to solve the problem of the international political organisation of these peoples. As early as 1818, he communicated to the Argentine Martín de Pueyrredón that the Americans would hasten to establish with the greatest interest an American pact that "presents America to the world with an aspect of majesty and greatness without example in the ancient nations". The formation of a political League of peoples that had previously been subjected to Spanish power stands out in the Bolivarian ideology, and nowhere is there a prevalence in this international ideology of a geographical criterion in the sense of including all of America from Alaska to Tierra del Fuego, but rather a Cultural Criterion, which excluded Anglo-Saxon America. A North American scholar tells us:

"In vain can one scrutinize Bolívar's writings in search of an approval of the attitude of Colombia, Mexico and

Central America to extend the invitation to the United States... He (Bolívar) did not trust much in the protection that the United States could provide, nor did he accept the pre-eminence in this Hemisphere, implicit in the Monroe Declaration".

In his work, "Bolívar and Inter-American Relations", Méndez Pereira affirms that in "Washington a great opposition to the Panama project arose and Congress resolved that the United States should not become a party with the South American Republics or with any of them".

In his essay, under the name of "Intimacies of the Panama Congress of 1826", Don Ernesto de J. Castillero tells us the following:

"The United States received an invitation from the Colombian government, dated 7 October 1824... The instructions that the State Department gave to its Delegates to act in the Panama Congress included, among other things, not to compromise the neutrality of the United States in the conflicts of the Latin republics with Spain; to defend at all costs the freedom of the seas and to reject any attempt at European colonisation on the Continent except in the case of Cuba and Puerto Rico, which the United States preferred as Spanish colonies rather than being incorporated into the free nations of Colombia and Mexico whose governments wanted to liberate both islands from Spanish rule... the North American observers also brought instructions to oppose the recognition of the Republic of Haiti".

As can be observed, the Congress that Bolívar conceived had enthusiastic adherents and covert or open opponents, but the criterion prevailed that it was necessary to establish, for the good of these Hispanic American nations, a solid political and cultural union, with ties in the social and religious traditions brought from Spain. The concept was imposed that the aforementioned League should have at its disposal certain supranational instructions with sufficient powers to take internal security measures for defence purposes without undermining the autonomy of each republic or nation. The system should have its own headquarters in which all countries would be equidistant for purposes of convenience, practicality and rapid transfer from one site to another. These nations should remain united at all times and circumstances, resorting to dialogue to settle possible differences, as indeed arose later. Likewise, Liberator Bolívar thought that none of the nations that made up this vast community could make agreements with other countries without considering the opinion and point of view of the others, especially if those countries attempted or could attempt against Hispanic American security. As an ideal that has not yet been realised, Bolívar thought of something like a continental citizenship, a Hispanic American citizenship that would suppress the differences between the different nationalities, because after all, they all formed part of the same conglomerate united by social and religious tradition, by language and by intellectual culture, including idiosyncrasy, as a psychological inheritance from the Spanish. Bolívar sought to establish in this Congress the bases for a preferential type of trade policy in which there would be a kind of common market, thus avoiding methods of discrimination against products manufactured in Latin America.

As an indispensable matter, the creation of an armed force integrated by contingents that each country could contribute according to its internal capacities or potential resources became peremptory. Bolívar's thinking not only consulted political and military aspects; it also took into account social problems such as slavery. Méndez Pereira affirms in relation to the issues of the 1826 Congress that England became fearful when it learned of its preparations and cites O'Leary in that the Panama Congress created the fear that monarchy would be proscribed in America and "exaggerated principles of freedom would be propagated". Raúl Porras Barrenechea, referring to the English envoy, Mr Edward James Dawkings, says that he was in the Panama Congress, "a kind of rigid and solemn stone guest who did not officially open his mouth for any matter". Although Bolívar had thought of resorting to England in the realisation of the future Panama Canal.

According to Méndez Pereira, the United States adopted, with respect to this international meeting, an attitude of indolence towards the independence cause of Hispanic America and to the possible jealousy that the presence of an English delegation in this Inter-American Conclave could arouse in the Washington government. English and North Americans made formal declarations about the importance of this Congress, but the facts came to belie these official expressions. Simón Bolívar himself was not present at these deliberations so as not to arouse suspicions of possible influences of his in the deliberations and agreements taken there. The aforementioned Congress held ten sessions and was closed, as we have already seen, on 5 July of the same year. The Treaty in question had 31 articles and we have outlined it in previous paragraphs. The only nation that signed it was Colombia, deciding that this Assembly of free countries would move to Tacubaya, Mexico, but with Bolívar's disapproval. The Tacubaya meeting failed due to a series of social anxieties, precarious civil administration, political instability, and unbridled power struggles between antagonistic groups interested in imposing their own criteria.

Professor Bonifacio Pereira J. tells us about the results of this Congress:

"The idea was so advanced for those days that it apparently failed. This is what happens with everything. We understand that they would not have understood Simón Bolívar in 1826. The Liberator failed. He threw to the four winds the seed that has not yet sunk into fertile ground. He spoke in the language of the future and that is why he believed he had ploughed in the sea. He was too far ahead of his historical present".

In reality, the Panama meeting of '26 was not a success and of its decisions the Liberator came to say that "its power will be a shadow and its decrees, advice nothing more". Nevertheless, the foundations of a new International Law were thus laid, based on arbitration, fraternal relations and the collective interest of nations in posterity. The Bolivarian ideal was not only rooted in his powerful and brilliant intuition, but in the very material needs of the peoples south of the Rio Grande. And so we have that in a conference given at the Bolivarian Society by Dr Juan Ernesto Rothe, Venezuelan ambassador to Panama in 1964, he came to maintain that Simón Bolívar can be considered as a precursor of Agrarian Reform in America, and for this he resorts to testimonies, letters and autobiographical documents of Bolívar, pointing out said author the three basic elements of current validity: land distribution, technical assistance (Bolivian Decree of 1820) and agricultural credit. These aspects of Bolivarian ideology are interesting to record, since the theme of the Panama Congress is thought of in purely political and military terms.

The disintegration of Gran Colombia was not a casual fact or the product of simple lust for power. At the bottom of this vast federation of peoples, antithetical elements were latent that compelled violence, political frenzy and social dissolution. The immensity of the Gran Colombian territory within which Panama was located, gave rise to all kinds of localisms, both political, geographical and economic. Despite all these peoples speaking the same language and professing the same religious faith, powerful economic interests were present, entrenched in old systems of privileges inherited from the colonial era. The ideological groups in conflict, liberals and conservatives (Bolivarians), translated in their broad lines the struggle of economic interests. The liberal element represented, more or less, the customs and way of life of the urban nuclei, a mercantile class, desirous of expanding much more the framework of colonial-type traditions; this same element aspired, in their respective countries, to a peace where it would be possible, without semi-feudal obstacles or impediments. They were the same ones who, according to Mariano Arosemena, "formed from their private fortunes the necessary funds for the payment of deserters" in 1821. For its part, the Conservative Party was identified with

Bolívar's dictatorial poses, not so much out of unconditional adherence to him, but because his figure and his prestige, his combative and iron spirit, accorded more with the traditional and colonialist spirit of the old landowners and, any form of progressive character.

We could even say that when Bolívar assumed the dictatorship, decreeing repression laws against "traitors and conspirators", he was being used involuntarily by an element that only saw in him a kind of screen for the defence of its own and traditional interests. Bolívar acted with sincerity and there is ample proof of this, but the groups that took shelter under his hero's halo took advantage of him to push forward plans such as wanting to convert him into the lifelong President of Gran Colombia. In the Liberator's conduct, clear contradictions can be seen: on the one hand, he approves the decisions of the Bolivarians to sabotage the Ocaña Convention, dominated by liberals, an event that occurred on 6 June 1828; on the other hand, he told Colombians that if he fulfilled his promises, they would be free and respected. But on the other hand, he issued decrees favouring popular education that contrasted with his acceptance in good faith of the omnipotent command that was offered to him. The conspiracy against Bolívar's life on the night of 25 September 1828 was one of the many episodes of Colombian life that highlighted the struggles between liberals, supporters of the federal system of government, and conservatives, defenders of a strong centralist administration that, point by point, translated the mentality of the Habsburgs when they dominated this part of the Western Hemisphere.

Based on what has been said, we can affirm that the dissensions within Gran Colombia were due, then, to facts not necessarily ideological. On 6 November 1829, a plural number of notable Panamanians, due to their social position, requested from the Liberator, among many things, to facilitate the development of enormous wealth as a source of public prosperity and to "declare the Isthmus a country of free trade with all the peoples of the earth, without prohibiting any kind of goods, fruits or productions". If this part of Gran Colombia asked for things like those mentioned, it is not surprising that a refusal to such a request, not only here, but in the other constituencies, had to favour as a natural consequence, a spirit of rebellion, a subversive activity against a fictitious political equality. Bolívar tried to stop this apocalyptic march, urging the Provinces to subordinate themselves to order for the sake of peace, dictating provisions in Cúcuta, decreeing amnesties in Puerto Cabello and pacifying, in short, public life. But the failure of the Ocaña Convention, dominated by passions and the attempt on Bolívar's life itself, the war between Peru and Colombia, the secession of Venezuela from Gran Colombia and despite the decision of the Admirable Congress of 1830 organizing the country's political life, the assassination of Antonio José de Sucre in Berruecos, the subsequent dictatorship of General Rafael Urdaneta, all conspired to bring about disintegrating convulsion and civil war.

The events that took place throughout the extent of the Gran Colombian territory occurred by virtue, then, of the mistrust, misgivings and fears based on facts unquestionably linked to the socio-political reality of the time. Such an enormous community of peoples within whose bosom the most contradictory interests were debated, could not bear the weight of events that produced a true trauma in the structure of these nations.

The government of José Sardá, a man who did not show affection towards the republican system, and rather a supporter of the monarchical form, preluded in the Isthmus the future dictatorship of Bolívar sponsored by Sardá himself, the General Commander, José Domingo Espinar and Dr Juan José Cabarcas, under the pretext of the failure of the Ocaña Convention and the well-known risks that this meant for public security, urging an "energetic remedy" (the dictatorship), which would have profound repercussions on the institutional life of the Isthmus. The struggle of interests between the class of landowners of conservative mentality who saw in Bolívar the representative of their goods, and the class of merchants and liberals of other criteria in economic and political matters, led the country to a precarious, unstable situation, in which Tomás Herrera himself and José Vallarino Jiménez were involved, who were accused of having figured as conspirators against the life of the Liberator. Historians Dr Florentino González ("Memories of the Era of Dictatorship") and Dr José María Samper ("Notes for History") have contributed to forming this erroneous idea about Herrera's participation in such an act. About Tomás Herrera that "nothing more inaccurate, however". And he also tells us:

"Happy the conspirators of 25 September, for at least from that ignominy they were saved. If Bolívar dies, all the conspirators would have been criminals; saved, posterity

condemns the crime, but grants mitigating circumstances to some of its authors, whom a republican delirium that degenerated into demagogic fury had deprived of the use of reason".

This episode and many more, such as the constant clashes between liberals and conservatives, the tension between regions, Bolívar's decision to abandon command, the election of Joaquín Mosquera as President and General Domingo Caicedo as Vice President, the general chaos, made the situation practically difficult in all the confines of Gran Colombia. But in Panama, with the departure of Sardá and the new administration of Colonel Fábrega, things seemed to be going quite well, when General José Domingo Espinar was appointed by Vice President Caicedo as General Commander of the Department of the Isthmus, one of his first acts being not to take the legal oath, as required, to take possession of the position, which foreshadowed not only his adherence to Bolívar but his firm decision to act outside the law, disobeying the order to abandon the recently acquired position by mandate of President Mosquera, to be replaced by General José Hilario López, and to go to take possession of the governorship of Veraguas. Espinar disobeyed these indications, despite the requirements of Tomás Herrera and Don Mariano Arosemena, supporters of the liberal group. Espinar's subsequent actions led to riots, pressures, violence, deportations, using the slogan that it was about restoring the rights of the Liberator and that the situation was propitious to push forward old separatist feelings rooted in the Isthmus for a long time.

All this foreshadowed in the local environment a new era for us and the separatist attempts of Panama in the decades that followed the year 1821. Relations between the Isthmus and Colombia began to show clear fissures, giving rise to doubts regarding the value that had been given to the annexationism of 28 November of the year 21. Castillero Calvo, in his essay, "The Hanseatic Movement of 1826" tells us:

"The Hanseatic reaction that occurred in the Isthmus as a consequence of the centralizing and dictatorial stimulus of the Bolivarian State, has not remained totally unpublished for our historiography... but this decisive chapter of our history has remained untouched".

He relates the economic failure of the union with Colombia, the frustrated attempts to obtain commercial franchises, as well as a way of not falling into economic ruin and not losing long-awaited prerogatives that were practically ignored and cunningly concealed by the central government in Bogotá, representative of Colombian mercantile groups. The Hanseatic purposes to which he refers were a reaction against the Bolivarian Statute which was, precisely, the antithesis of the desire for free trade advocated by the already known "Isthmian Circle", so combated by Espinar in his "Historical Summary". It is also revealed, according to a quote made from the Colombian historian, José María Quijano Wallis, that the Panamanians tried "the forbidden exaggeration of annexing themselves to Great Britain", adding later that powerful, rich groups requested protection from Great Britain from the English representation in Jamaica, an attempt frustrated by Espinar and which meant, says Castillero Calvo, "a momentary popular triumph", followed by other Hanseatic attempts sponsored by economically powerful and influential groups.

The case of the Panama Canal

What should have been a great project that would launch Panama as an independent country to be an important part of international trade, thanks to the approval of the construction of a canal by the French company of Ferdinand de Lesseps, became the worst nightmare that can happen to a newly constituted country.

The avid northern power of the United States had other plans: it wanted the Panama Canal for itself, and would achieve it with a few conspiracies.

The French company declared bankruptcy and in a short time the United States took control of the work, and what should have been a public tender in the eyes of the law ended up becoming an occupation without a declaration of war and without military invasion.

While the Panama Canal was being built, at the same time, the Americans were building a city for themselves at both ends of the canal, a small colony on the banks of the canal. And, as if that were not enough, they built military bases without asking permission and without asking for forgiveness, with the sole justification that these bases would serve to safeguard the security of the canal. This was one of the first infamies of the many that the United States would commit in the young 20th century.

From what should have been a 50-50 business, the United States had total control over the canal whose main asset was its narrow isthmus, which separated the Pacific Ocean from the Caribbean Sea.

Our main geographical feature and our best strategic advantage, which is the Isthmus of Panama, served for Panamanians to become an American colony for almost a century. Panama was their first experiment in military colonialism of the 20th century.

What should have been a mere commercial contract between a country and a company became a treaty with clear inequalities and totally rigged between two countries, to turn us into an American colony at the beginning of our history as a republic. A complete city and military bases should never have appeared in the specifications.

It was said at that time that, to build the canal, tropical diseases had to be eliminated or eradicated. But the curious thing is that in 400 years that the Spaniards were building cities in the middle of jungles and forests, they never told in their chronicles anything about such diseases that were transmitted through mosquitoes, rather it was the Europeans who brought diseases that decimated a large number of the indigenous population.

A very important clarification must be made: Gorgas was not a scientist, nor a researcher or academic, much less an epidemiologist or infectologist, he was only an army doctor.

During the construction of the canal, the United States did not even take Panamanians into account, opening and mining their own mountains, and neither during operations were Panamanians taken into account to be permanent employees. Perhaps the gringos thought that Panamanians were troglodytes incapable of learning a trade or labour. And thus they imposed a labour regime of racial discrimination, which would be an apartheid.

The American bases in Panamanian territory would be among the first bases that the United States established throughout the 20th century, taking advantage of any military conflict in which they participated, as they would put a military base there as a symbol of supremacy and subjugation. With victory in World War II and the Cold War, the United States would consider themselves the masters of the world and would rub it in the faces of other countries that, without them, victory would have been for the Axis forces, led by the Nazis. For this reason, they declared themselves with the right to occupy any country and establish military bases, violating its sovereignty and all international law.

The EU, the UN and the US should sit down to negotiate the withdrawal of US military bases since the end of World War II, because it seems they do not intend to withdraw, they claim their war booty in perpetuity. The same goes for Japan and South Korea. And the withdrawal of the military presence in Iraq and Afghanistan should also be negotiated.

There is something surprising: the financial capacity and the armament deployment to maintain so many military bases in all parts of the world. A true waste of money in the name of maintaining hegemony.

We know that many US military operations came out of the canal bases, with the Southern Command, and not necessarily for the defense of the canal. These military bases were built only to have a permanent military presence in Central and South America.

I have already deciphered why the United States participates in so many military conflicts, the vast majority of which are avoidable. It is due to the ego of their presidents and the lobby of the military industry, who flatter the presidents in turn to initiate or intervene in military conflicts and thus remind them that they will enter history like generals or Roman emperors who also sought military honours and glories. But with the difference that the presidents are never at the front of their armies directing their troops, they achieve victory from their refrigerated offices or sheltered from secret bunkers and, in turn, the military industry takes a juicy profit from the military spending of the US army.

Any company that wins a military tender would become a multimillionaire overnight. And this without including that, when they sell obsolete weaponry to third world countries, they also obtain juicy profits

With the ideology of UELA, any aerial bombing against civilians should be considered a crime against humanity for attacking unarmed civilians and causing numerous innocent deaths, and thus it will be denounced in international forums and organizations.

The interest of the United States in building the interoceanic canal

In 1901, the Hay-Pauncefote Treaty was signed between the United States and the United Kingdom. This agreement eliminated the Clayton-Bulwer and left the United States with authority over Central America; especially, free to build the canal.

The United States was in the era of its maximum expansion of political, economic and military power. In 1898, without any reason, it declared war on Spain, already weakened due to all the conspiracies perpetrated by the United Kingdom for 400 years, and took control of Cuba, Puerto Rico and the Philippines from it.

The Caribbean became a great American and British lake. For the United States, it was its Manifest Destiny, as indicated by its Big Stick policy.

Immediate consequences of the canal treaty with the United States

1. Panama became an American colony without invasion (the invasion had to wait 85 more years) and without shedding a drop of blood (now there are mass graves and disappeared persons).

2. The United States had total and absolute control over the operations and administration of the canal. Panama did not receive an equitable benefit from the canal's benefits as an equal partner, but rather received only crumbs.

3. The United States did not take Panamanians into account as a workforce.

4. There was constant interference in Creole politics by the US Government.

5. Without a doubt, the Hay-Bunau Varilla treaty, signed on November 18, 1903, just two weeks after Panama became an independent and sovereign republic, was a jewel of international law.

Some notes from the book "The History of Panama" by Prof. Luis H. Tapia

The United States and the United Kingdom were the nations most interested in acquiring control over the Central American regions to build a trans-isthmic canal, because it would facilitate their expansion and consolidate their political and economic power over America and other parts of the world, as happened with Gibraltar and the Suez Canal, under British rule.

The United Kingdom invaded territories to the north of Nicaragua, Honduras and Guatemala (Belize emerges), and the United States consolidated its expansion over Mexico and California, annexing vast territories for the Confederates.

This expansive interest of the United States had originated since 1823, with President James Monroe's declaration that "America" was a matter for Americans. It is the so-called Monroe Doctrine, the oldest fascist doctrine, and still in force.

In 1846, the Mallarino-Bidlack Treaty or General Treaty of Peace, Friendship and Commerce (United States with New Granada) was signed to partially curb British dominion.

But later, in 1850, the United States signed the Clayton-Bulwer Treaty with the United Kingdom, where both make a non-aggression pact and indicate that, if the canal were to be built through Central America, it would be jointly with the same privileges for both parties and without either of them colonizing the area.

The Gold Rush

After the discovery of valuable gold deposits in the Sacramento Valley (California) in 1848, the news spread throughout the world, which caused a human avalanche towards that region.

The shortest and fastest route to cross the eastern United States to the Pacific coast of California would be through Panama: using the Chagres River channel in Colón and then on mule back until reaching Panama City, where to take a ship to San Francisco.

This route was the old Spanish colonial road crossing, but given the high traffic of expeditionaries and adventurers, it was an expensive, painful and dangerous task.

The construction of the trans-isthmian railroad

The urgency to accelerate the trans-isthmian route produced the idea of building a railroad. For this, an

American company got a contract with the Government of New Granada: the Stephens-Paredes contract.

There were many setbacks and a high cost in human lives. However, the work was inaugurated on January 28, 1855.

It is estimated that more than 12,000 people may have died in the construction of the railroad. Cholera and malaria killed many workers.

The construction of the railroad by an American company was used by the United States Government to carry out military interventions on the isthmus both in 1856 and between the period from 1861 to 1885, supposedly to maintain order among the adventurers who were going to California.

British intervention was also felt on the isthmus. In 1870, English-speaking West Indians caused disturbances and the death of the mayor in the town of Taboga. In 1883, English subjects caused incidents in the town of Culebra.

The French canal and the American interest in the interoceanic route

The canal is the clearest manifestation of the extraordinary geographical position of the Isthmus of Panama. Its importance was already manifested in the time of Pedrarias Dávila, founder of Panama City in 1519. The Camino Real de Cruces was created, which was one of the historical routes of the isthmus that connected the Caribbean Sea and the Pacific Ocean, through which almost all goods from the Pacific passed to Spain. It was the shortest route across the continent to cross the two seas.

At the beginning of the 19th century, in 1815, Bolívar proposed the construction of a canal through Panama in his famous "Jamaica Letter".

In 1878 the "contract" for the construction of the interoceanic canal was signed, between the signatories Lucién Napoleón Bonaparte Wyse, president of the "societé civile" and Eustorgio Salgar, secretary of foreign relations of Colombia.

Engineer Bonaparte Wyse sold the contract to the Universal Interoceanic Canal Company, directed by Count Ferdinand De Lesseps, who had achieved worldwide success with the construction of the Suez Canal.

The work began in 1880, and in 1882 the excavations began, but "soon" the "work failed" mainly due to lack of funds.

Poor administration and misappropriation of funds gave rise to one of the most famous international scandals, the Panama Scandal, which turned the name of Panama into a synonym for theft and robbery.

The great conspiracy of the French canal

Did the construction of the French canal fail or were there powerful interests that wanted the project to fail in order to later take control of the work?

According to history, the failure of the Universal Interoceanic Canal Company was due to:

1. **The embezzlement and theft of monetary funds, as a consequence of the enormous corruption that was destroying the French republic**. How a company with the experience gained in administration, operations and resource management that had just successfully built the Suez Canal, which until that moment was the largest engineering work of the 19th century, where it had gained high prestige, is going in such a "short time" to run out of funds and become involved in a scandalous handling of misappropriation and theft of funds due to the corruption of the French Government. This work was not financed with funds from the French Government, therefore, the French Government, corrupt or not, had nothing to do with the financing of the work. Which banks financed the work? Was there a bond involved? Was there any arbitration? Was the Government of Colombia compensated? The Suez Canal was the largest engineering work of the 19th century, carried out by Ferdinand de Lesseps' company. This work, built in Egypt, united the Mediterranean with the Red Sea. The construction was a complete success, and Lesseps was filled with glory and fame. Although the canal was built by the French, it would soon pass under British control, since Egypt was under British rule and the English banks that financed the work put obstacles in the way of the Egyptian Government and, in this way, the United Kingdom would take control of the route. Controlling the Suez Canal route for the British was to take hegemonic control of the Middle East and the Mediterranean and, in

turn, control of maritime trade, especially oil trade, which was beginning its boom.

If the French canal were to be built in Panama, France and Colombia would have control over the route between the Atlantic and the Pacific and this would not suit the interests of the United States to dominate in America.

2. **Technical errors, such as the total ignorance of the geological characteristics of the isthmus**. Engineering is the technique of executing on the fly. Every engineering work poses constant obstacles and unforeseen events. There will be technical errors in any project and more so in this enormous work. French engineers were of very high capacity and preparation, so they surely could have found optimal and scientific solutions to the problems and challenges that the work could present. Likewise, they could have asked for technical assistance from other experts worldwide. In addition, the Americans only needed dynamite to make their way.

3. **Yellow fever and the deadly climate of Panama**. Why thirty years ago, during the construction of the trans-isthmian railroad, there were no yellow fever epidemics, nor were the areas where the railroad route would be sanitized. How is it that 400 years ago Spaniards and Portuguese crossed jungle areas in the midst of vermin and clouds of mosquitoes, as described in their chronicles, and no European was affected or infected by any disease caused by any mosquito except for bruises due to bites? On the contrary. Europeans brought diseases to the New World that the immune system of the natives was not prepared

to defend against some viruses and bacteria. A native could die from a simple cold. Yellow fever is native to Africa and not to America. How did it arrive just when the construction of the French Canal was beginning and only where the excavations were being made? This disease and its treatment were not known in Panama.

How Dr. William Gorgas, a United States Army doctor, who arrived in Panama from Cuba learned the treatment there after treating patients with yellow fever in that country, was able to eradicate the epidemic to almost 0% of those affected after sanitation in the areas where the canal would be built by the United States. Curiously, the rest of the country was not sanitized or fumigated, but there were also no yellow fever affected in the rest of the country. All this seems very suspicious and even worthy of a deeper investigation by independent historians, since it was calculated that between 1881 and 1902 there were 6,280 deaths from yellow fever, malaria, dysentery, tuberculosis and pneumonia, while other calculations raise the deaths to 22,000.

According to history, Dr. Gorgas realized that the larvae of the Aedes aegypti mosquito (as its name indicates, it is a mosquito native to Africa) were bred in the trays placed on the legs of the patients' beds, supposedly to prevent ants from climbing up to the beds through them. This whole story is complete nonsense, since a clean, disinfected and fumigated room would not have to have ants, and ants do not climb into beds unless they detect sweet residues, whether jam, honey, etc. And, thirdly, the worst thing was to place water in the trays when they could very well have placed vinegar or alcohol, since stagnant water is a source of contamination and infections. In Panama, the Aedes aegypti mosquito transmits classic and haemorrhagic dengue, zika and chikungunya. Only in 2019 there were four deaths, but there has been no outbreak of yellow fever.

As for the **deadly climate of Panama**, in 1519 the city of Panama was founded with the same climatic conditions with which the canal was built. There was no need to do any sanitation or mass vaccinations to control plagues or contagious diseases due to any pandemic. In 1671, the city of Panama was sacked by the Welsh pirate Henry Morgan on orders from the English crown, so it was moved to a new location, where it is today. If Panama had a deadly climate as one of the adverse factors for the construction of the canal, there would not have been the conditions for the foundation and then the expansion of Panama City, just as the Americans would not have built a city-state with military bases within the margins of the interoceanic canal.

The other option of building an interoceanic canal through Nicaragua

Nicaragua was never used by the Spanish as a route to cross from one ocean to another for the transfer of goods. The construction of the trans-isthmian railway affirmed that the route through Panama was the most viable, and this was later confirmed by the construction of the French canal.

The proposal to build a canal through Nicaragua was only a ploy or strategy to pressure the newly formed country of Panama to make a treaty to the convenience and advantage of the United States.

A “treaty”, and not a contract, as it should have been, like the railroad contract and the French canal construction contract.

The United States did not conduct a technical or feasibility study to see if it was possible to build a canal through Nicaragua.

UNITED WE WILL BE STRONGER. THE DEVELOPMENT AND CONSOLIDATION OF UELA

The great challenges and at the same time the great obstacles for the creation of the Union of Latin American States

1. Unite our territories (but each State would maintain its sovereignty and independence) and our economies (that all member States have the same economic doctrine and model) giving it the name Union of Latin American States. The desire of Latin American countries to create a union. The obstacle is that some countries or the majority do not see a benefit in this union based on mutual respect, mutual benefit and economic and political unity.

2. Total independence from the capitalist and communist yokes that subjugate Latin American peoples. The obstacle lies in the fact that the great de facto powers do not wish or see inconveniences in losing their status quo and their good relations with the hegemonic States.

3. Implement a new socio-economic, political and legal ideology in the society of Latin American nations. To have real independence from these economic doctrines that subjugate us, it is necessary to develop our own social, legal, economic and political doctrine. A doctrine based on cooperation, solidarity and commitment.

4. Put an end to any totalitarian and populist regime. Any national, whether civilian, political or military, collaborator of foreign intelligence agencies must immediately resign from their disloyal service to favour foreign powers. If they continue working for these agencies, they will be accused of high treason and condemned to be shot. In the case of being a foreigner, they must leave any Latin American country within one month; if they continue working for these agencies and are detected in espionage, they will be captured and condemned as a death row inmate and shot.

5. Businessmen who have invested their capital in international stock exchanges should withdraw their investments as soon as possible. And withdraw their funds from foreign banks. One of UELA's priorities in the following five years will be economic equalisation and monetary equality or common currency for member countries.

Capitalism: Wealth and fortunes for reduced oligarchic elites. Inequality, poverty and exploitation for the salaried class.

Communism: Totalitarianism, persecution, repression and slavery for the proletarian class.

Latin America will change when every citizen wishes their neighbour to be well or even better than oneself. When we support and help each other as neighbours. This also translates to the States of Latin America. This way we will avoid violence, which is the worst evil that gnaws at us. From here will emerge peaceful citizens and honest and honourable politicians.

Official languages of UELA

The official languages of UELA will be Spanish (Castilian) and Portuguese, which will be used in meetings and sessions. In schools and universities, English and French should also be taught as a third and fourth language, but they will not be official languages. Greek and Latin can be studied in the academic curriculum of schools and universities.

Civic-political-military pact

All Latin American States that wish to belong to UELA must also deliver a civic-military-political pact.

This pact must reflect the agreements or commitments that must be fulfilled.

For this, they must hold a great council or town hall and express their demands and the agreements they have reached. And this pact must be endorsed in the Assembly of each country.

On the prohibition of trade and use of firearms

It is imperative and extremely urgent that Latin American countries, through their legislative and judicial bodies, prohibit the importation, trade and use of firearms.

For more than a century and a half, Latin American society has been bleeding in acts of violence, criminality and even massacres perpetrated almost by a common denominator, which is the use of firearms, filling our families with mourning, pain and helplessness. And turning hundreds of citizens into criminals and murderers.

Prohibiting the importation, trade and use of firearms will not be an easy task. The large and powerful lobbies where firearms are manufactured and that control this trade manage to bend high officials of the different organs of the State through extortion or blackmail so that their businesses produce millionaire dividends at the cost of the blood that is shed daily, and the news massively promote these crimes to cause indifference or indolence in the population.

The use of weapons of all kinds only serves to incite violence, criminality, homicide, the formation of gangs, guerrilla groups and even terrorist groups, which obtain their power from them.

The prohibition of the importation, trade and use of firearms will bring about living in quieter and safer cities and neighbourhoods.

Only the Armed Forces will be able to use firearms and the Police will use firearms and non-lethal weapons as use of force by constitutional order.

The sale of toy weapons for children should also be prohibited, as they can incite them to violence.

The legislation should not only prohibit all export, smuggling, trade and use of firearms, but also sharp weapons, and will impose harsh sanctions or penalties for those who fail to comply.

Reconciliation between the military, politicians and citizens in UELA member states

Mentioning the word "military" or "militarism" in the history of Latin American peoples is synonymous with dictatorships, systematised persecution, disappearances, torture, rape, abuse of power, narco-dictatorships and illegal enrichment, in other words, a series of disproportionate vices that have left mourning, pain, poverty, resentment and open wounds caused by the defence institutions created to do the exact opposite.

The purpose of UELA is unity, but there will be no unity if there is no reconciliation between the military, politicians and citizens.

There will be a truce between the military and civil society. All military bases will be removed from cities and only police detachments will be allowed.

No military or police officer may, while on duty or not, threaten or intimidate a civilian.

The military will not be able to attend civilian social centres unless they are invited. The military will have their own social centres.

Only in the event that anarchy or civil disobedience spreads can the army intervene, as long as the constitution allows it, and the order will be given by the Senate or the Assembly.

It is reiterated that, in the constitutive charter, UELA will establish that any attempt to usurp political power by a military or civilian coup will be overthrown immediately by the military coalition and democracy will be immediately restored. And much less will the interference in the internal affairs of foreign powers be allowed.

UELA member states must, by constitutional mandate, prohibit the Armed Forces of their countries from violating or trampling on citizens, since, by constitutional power, citizens are the supreme sovereigns of the State and the Armed Forces.

But that or those citizens who are friends of street violence, civil anarchy or assassinate police or military will be punished with the death penalty.

A great Latin American military coalition

Latin America has been built thanks to the vision of many great military men, today considered heroes and founders of many of our countries, but unfortunately, during the last two centuries, the military has interrupted the constitutional order and have become tyrants and dictators of the peoples they once promised to protect and defend. The high commands of the Armed Forces only live for greed, arbitrariness, boasting and privileges. They are far from assuming their historical role of hoisting the flag of our great founders.

If Latin America united its armed forces, the result would be one of the largest. But they need comprehensive reengineering and one of the most effective organisational policies. Each country will have its own Armed Forces for its internal security and defence, and will cede troops and military equipment for the formation of the LAF (Latin American Armed Forces). The troops that are voluntarily ceded will receive additional payment for their services in the LAF. Military academies and military bases will be created to train and house this joint force.

As for security establishments, such as Police, Migration, Customs, these institutions will be independent for each country, but an exchange system can be made for better integration and to homologate systems.

UELA will declare itself a non-aligned organisation. We will not be allies of any foreign power, we will not be enemies of any foreign power, and we will not be satellites of any foreign power.

This implies never again being the backyard of any foreign power and having the military capacity to defend our territory from any threat from a foreign hegemonic power.

Military and Security System agents of Latin America can only be trained and educated within the countries that make up UELA.

The Armed Forces of Latin American countries, LAF, must create a military industry so as not to buy or depend on foreign armament, much less allow military or security advice from any foreign power. Unless, for reasons of immediate security, defence and security treaties can be concluded with other nations that are considered not hostile to Latin American interests.

Modernise the Armed Forces of the States that make up UELA

One of the advantages of creating a military coalition of UELA countries would be the homologation and modernisation of the entire military apparatus, both in armament and equipment, communication and operational organisation.

Purposes of the modernisation of the Armed Forces:

1.Defend the Union from any threat or aggression by any belligerent State or external enemy force.

The Latin American commands

The Armed Forces of Latin American countries, LAF, will form a military coalition to defend and prevent military invasion by any foreign empire. The commands will be military bases of the three forces, Army, Navy and Air Force, formed by all nationalities of the States of the Union of Latin American States.

The commands would be formed as follows:

1. The Amazon Command (military and scientific).
2. The Antarctic Command (military and scientific).
3. The Central Atlantic Command.
4. The Canal-Caribbean Command.
5. The Canal-Pacific Command.
6. The Caribbean Command.
7. The South Pacific Command.
8. The Central Pacific Command.
9. The North Pacific Command.

These commands must have docks, airports, hangars, training centres and a very well-conditioned nearby community so that the military are with their families. The service of the military in these commands can be two years. Although it will also be allowed to make a military career in the LAF. Also build a great Navy to protect and defend the immense coasts of the Union, both in the Pacific, and in the Atlantic, the Gulf of Mexico and the Caribbean Sea.

The war conflicts between Latin American countries

If we compare the war history of Europe with the war history between Latin American countries, we see that Europe has been bleeding for almost 2000 years between neighbouring peoples, invasions, internal wars and, finally, as the scene of the two world wars. But today, and thanks to tireless and praiseworthy diplomatic work, Europe enjoys an era of peace thanks to the creation of the European Union. Although there are pending tasks, such as addressing the problem of the Balkans and the countries of the former Yugoslavia, relations with the Baltic countries, its relations with Turkey and, especially, with the powerful State of Russia.

Although Latin American countries have not had many military conflicts with each other in two hundred years, unfortunately we have bled in internal wars, whether through civil wars, rebellions to overthrow a regime or the pure repression of brutal military dictatorships.

If Europe, with its long history of military conflicts, its very marked nationalisms, its multilingualism and the melting pot of all political and economic ideologies, has decided to work together, then it would be much easier for Latin America to do so.

Although there was a war known as the War of the Triple Alliance and the War of the Pacific between Peru, Chile and Bolivia, I believe that these pages should be turned and we should dream of a profound and definitive reconciliation. The whole world benefits from us being divided. But once we were a single territory, under the crown of Spain, or rather, we were two viceroyalties of Spain and the immense Brazil was part of Portugal. An interesting fact very much in favour of the union between the Hispanic American countries and Brazil is that Spain and Portugal have had parallel histories in a way, since they were once a single kingdom and managed to colonise the American lands, as they were maritime powers thanks to brave explorers and wise navigators.

We have the right and even the great opportunity to become a great political, economic, commercial and military coalition. It may be a call from our destiny to fulfil such a noble mission.

Immediately, the world will stop calling us third world countries. We must close ranks to achieve this great accomplishment, as was the vision of the Liberator Simón Bolívar. He dreamed of creating Gran Colombia, as he saw uniting all of Latin America, except Brazil, as too ambitious.

But now, as sovereign and independent countries, we have the mature conscience to consider a great Latin American coalition between Spanish-speaking countries and Brazil, since, although it is true that the history of Hispanic America is not the same as that of Brazil, it is very parallel.

Today, Hispanic American countries and Brazil are part of many international organisations such as the UN and the OAS, and of many regional cooperation organisations. There is all the diplomatic and organisational experience to sit down and project and develop a definitive integration model such as a Union of Latin American States.

Definitive separation between the political class and the security and defence establishments

A definitive separation between the Armed Forces and the executive power, or rather, the president of the republic, should be proposed.

The Armed Forces cannot be left under the command or orders of the parties in power.

The proposal is to keep the Armed Forces and security establishments separate under the command of the executive, with the purpose that politicians do not interfere in exclusively security and defence matters and at the same time the military will not be able to interfere in purely political matters. Therefore, the armed bodies will not be able to receive orders or instructions from the president or any government official. Similarly, presidents or the Minister of Defence will not be able to receive orders or instructions from the armed bodies.

We could say that the Armed Forces would become autonomous entities and their prohibitions, rights, responsibilities and privileges will be under constitutional mandate.

Coordination between military and politicians will be done through a consultation body that could be called the Security and Defence Council formed by a group of military experts (members of the General Staff) and another group of politicians (members of the Ministry of Defence) experts in international politics and strategy. This Security and Defence Council will meet every week to share or exchange classified and sensitive information for national security and based on the results of these meetings, public policies on security and defence will be established.

The Armed Forces and the Ministry of Defence will be at the same hierarchical level.

Constitutionally, the Armed Forces will be able to:

1. Defend the State from any threat or aggression by a belligerent State or external enemy force.

2. Not intervene in exclusively political matters and not allow politicians to interfere in exclusively security and defence matters.

3. Not become a repressive body or instigator of citizens or the people, who are the sovereigns of the State.

Military academies in the last year of training

Cadets who reach their last year of academic studies in their different countries and in their different branches must complete their studies in an academy where they will be with all the final year cadets from all the countries that make up UELA.

This final year academy aims to achieve coexistence and cultural exchange among all cadets and to create in the best possible way a certain camaraderie among colleagues that remains throughout the rest of their careers.

All types of rivalries or regionalist conflicts between cadets will be prohibited. If these bad practices occur, they will be sanctioned with expulsion and the person involved will be discharged.

These usual practices will be completely prohibited as a method of military training in military and police academies:

1. Physical abuse.
2. Psychological harassment.
3. Moral arbitrariness.
4. Humiliation and insult.

Neutrality treaty with other powers

Once UELA achieves the long-awaited independence from the American and British powers, it will obtain its economic, financial, commercial, industrial, political, military and cultural independence. A neutrality treaty must be immediately agreed with these highly belligerent, conspiratorial and usurping powers, especially in matters of espionage, intelligence and non-military intervention, specifically with:

a. The United States, a treaty to demilitarise Guantánamo in Cuba.

b. With the United Kingdom, a treaty to demilitarise the Malvinas or Falkland Islands in the South Atlantic of Argentina.

US or British nationals living within UELA

Nationals from these countries or those who want to settle in UELA will not receive any discriminatory treatment or receive any treatment that threatens their honour and dignity. They will be treated as citizens in the country where they want to settle.

Financial institutions

UELA must not for any reason request any type of loans or financial aid from either the World Bank or the IMF.

It must not give in to any type of consultancy offers, much less to their threats, often reflected in economic crises, hyperinflation and intelligence services working on how to eliminate obstacles and anyone who opposes their well-defined plans.

UELA member states that produce oil should leave OPEC and create their own organisation and trade with their own currencies.

Latin America should no longer export its precious metals, but create large reserves of gold, silver and copper and strengthen its sovereign financial systems against foreign banking. Our mining resources have been taken for almost more than a century. This reserve must remain in state banks and cannot be sold or ceded to any natural or legal person, or to any foreign State.

The reserve of foreign exchange in UELA member countries must be under the control of state central banks.

Economic sanctions by the United States

The interesting thing about US economic sanctions on an economically weak country is not so much that it sanctions it, but that it also sanctions countries that trade with the sanctioned country. Thus, it attacks the sovereignty of other States, which it simply intends to ignore because it considers itself the world power that governs the world with total providence. The United States cannot interfere in the trade of other countries.

The United States, since the second half of the 20th century, has violated supreme norms of international law. Its intelligence agencies systematically order the assassination of scientists, intellectuals, activists opposed to their war policies or who are against their liberal capitalist mercantilist doctrine. Its revenge is implacable and insatiable against anyone who dares to contradict or rebuke it for its errors and mistakes.

The Latin American Development Bank (LDB)

It will be a bank created with state funds from all Latin American countries with the purpose of cutting all financial aid from international organisations such as the International Monetary Fund, the Inter-American Development Bank or the World Bank. With low-interest loans, it will be exclusive to quell crises or emergencies. It must also be achieved at all costs that the central banks of each country are state-owned. Another function of the LDB will be to equate the currencies of all Latin American countries and that they have the same purchasing value, regardless of the country, and will have as a great project the creation of a single currency for UELA.

UELA before other international organisations

UELA will be the highest organisation at the Latin American level. No Latin American State that is part of it may join international organisations without its consent. And if UELA considers it necessary to be part of an international organisation, it will be so as a bloc, but through a representative of UELA.

The international scenario of UELA before other countries

UELA's international relations will be based on mutual respect and reciprocal collaboration with the rest of the countries. No country will be treated as a chess piece on the global geopolitical board, nor will we allow ourselves to be manipulated as pawns by any of the hegemonic powers.

The great natural resources of Latin America

Many Latin American countries are oil producers. A Latin American organisation of oil producers must be created and oil companies must be nationalised to commercialise oil only among Latin American countries with their own local currency. This should be done the same with mining. No foreign company will be able to exploit oil, gas, minerals, wood or other natural resources.

Prohibit all extraction of gold, silver or any precious metal through concessions to national or foreign mining companies. The extraction of these metals will be exploited exclusively by state companies.

Prohibit the export of gold, silver or any precious metal of great value extracted within the territory of the Union.

Create the Gold Reserve Bank and the Silver Reserve Bank to conserve these precious metals as an economic reserve.

Latin America and its industrial and technological barrier

Among the greatest challenges for Latin America will be to create its own computer and digital industry, design and manufacture its cell phones, computers, servers, etc. And develop its own Internet and its applications, develop its own land, sea and air transport industry. It will also be important to develop its own telecommunications industry.

Brain drain to developed countries

Developed countries are happy to attract brains or talents from third world countries, offering them good salaries and better opportunities than those they consider their countries of origin can offer them.

With the foundation of UELA, this will change. The best intellectual talents and the gifted in all scientific areas will be recruited to work in their own countries so that everything they develop is for the benefit of their countries. Although they will be able to study in developed countries and share their experience in important international congresses, their field of work will be their country of origin or within the UELA area. A search for all brains around the world will also have to be carried out so that they also work in favour of their Latin American countries.

Once brilliant minds are detected, from a young age they must have preferential treatment and provide them with the necessary facilities for their studies and academic preparation, and accompany them through tutors and psychologists throughout their training. Although they will be able to study at the best universities in the world, they must practice their professions within the territory that makes up UELA and they must be given support in whatever they need to carry out their scientific work, either with help from foundations or with government assistance itself.

Work will be done on a search project in schools or even much earlier in kindergartens for children who are gifted in talents for science, arts and sports and other areas of knowledge.

Give them and their parents special treatment, pay for all their studies that will be under a special programme. If the boys or girls are from humble backgrounds, they will be given all the comfort they require, both them and their families. Once they become of legal age, they will be given the opportunity to work in the areas they wish to develop.

Create a "Silicon Valley" and develop scientific and technological clusters

Develop a cluster of companies dedicated to innovation and the development of new technologies.

UELA could develop areas for the forefront of scientific and technological research.

These clusters would be created through public-private partnerships. They would be large structures to house all types of research centres, laboratories and even shelters for workers and researchers.

Three types of research and innovation areas will be established:

1. For exact, natural and applied sciences.
2. For social and human sciences.
3. For agricultural sciences and agro-industries, forest engineering, environmental, zoology and botany.
4. For engineering applied to industry and technological innovation.

They will be located in the three regions of UELA: one in North America, one in Central America and the Caribbean, and the other in South America.

The innovations and applications developed in these centres will be for the use and benefit of all UELA members.

UELA and nuclear energy

UELA will not develop or purchase nuclear weapons, but it will try to master nuclear energy for energy purposes such as carrying out nuclear plant projects to provide electrical energy and use the latest technology in terms of safety and environmental protection. The survival of humanity will not be put at risk due to belligerent desires.

To compensate for these projects, massive forest reforestation projects and the decontamination of rivers, lakes and coasts will be developed.

Nuclear technology will be used only to produce energy in large quantities for the benefit of the peoples. Latin America must catch up in terms of nuclear production to have the capacity to build safe nuclear reactors.

Great efforts will be made in research and development to make nuclear energy more friendly and prevent radioactive catastrophes.

Nuclear energy will not be used for military purposes and there will be no trade with countries that possess nuclear weapons or that traffic in radioactive metals for military or terrorist purposes.

UELA and its programme towards the space and astronautical race

That among all the member countries of UELA they manage to develop a programme for the conquest of space and reach a scientific, technological and industrial level capable of matching the countries that participate in the concert of space and astronautical adventure, would be one of the greatest achievements that could be reached with the coordination of its greatest and brightest minds in all areas of science and engineering and also have the support and advice of other countries that have achieved high development in space missions and research on the secrets of the universe.

Create a merchant fleet among all UELA member states

To be able to develop one of the largest and most important merchant fleets in the world and build the most modern shipyards for the construction of the most advanced merchant ships and use a common flag or registry.

Our cultural manifestations

Latin Americans are very prone to celebrate, party, squander on amusements and celebrations. Severe adjustments must be made to our behaviour in terms of how we have fun: we must reduce by half the canteens, bars and nightclubs that generate violence and social depravity, reduce prostitution and pornography in all its forms and media, sanctioning these illicit activities with severe fines.

On the other hand, we must dedicate most of our time to reading, make greater efforts in university study and research, investing in state and private universities.

The Latin American Academy of Sciences and Arts

To avoid the almost dominant influence or foreign cultural alienation, a Latin American censorship organisation should be created to ensure the preservation of the customs and traditions of each Latin American people. Foreign films that do not contribute anything positive or go against the values of each people, music, fashion and foreign cable or TV television programmes that undermine the identity or distort the dignity of Latin American peoples must be avoided at all costs.

It will be essential and a priority to provide it with resources among all countries to develop scientific, technological, humanistic and artistic research. And an annual prize will be created for the most outstanding scientists and artists. For example: The Sarmiento Prize in Humanities, the von Humboldt Prize for Geography, the Darwin Prize for Biology, the Bello Prize for Letters, the Ingenieros Prize for Philosophy, the García Márquez Prize for Literature, Mistral Prize for female poetry, Neruda Prize for male poetry, Baldor Prize for mathematics, Favaloro Prize for medicine, Blades Prize for composers, Romero Prize for peace or civic actions, Henríquez Ureña Prize for history, Juárez Prize for law and political sciences, Niemeyer Prize for architecture, Frida Prize for painting, etc. They would be awarded in the manner of the Nobel Prize. The nominees must be presented by each academy of sciences and arts of each country. The nominees must be Latin Americans who work inside or outside the union or foreigners who live and work within the union. There will also be annual awards for music in all its manifestations and awards for Latin American cinema.

We must create a great cultural wall against foreign powers that, thanks to their powerful and manipulative film industry, impose alien and controversial models of behaviour to our principles of coexistence, and thus stop the influence of these mass idols prefabricated by these powers.

University education in Latin America

A great objective would be to achieve that five of the Latin American universities can be within the lists of the thirty or forty best universities in the world. Specialised universities could be developed and in this way raise the standards of aptitudes and competencies, such as:

- University of Medical and Health Sciences.
- University of Exact Sciences and Applied Technologies.
- University of Natural Sciences and Geosciences.
- University of Social and Humanistic Sciences.
- University of Nautical, Port and Logistics Sciences.
- University of Agricultural, Forestry and Environmental Sciences.
- University of Arts and Cinematographic Sciences.
- University of Sports and Physical Training.

These universities should host students at Latin American and international level.

There are a series of therapies that should be dealt with in schools, patriotic service institutions, military academies, universities and any educational institution. Among them will be:

- Stress management.
- Anger management.
- Management of melancholy or depression.
- Treatment or therapy against some type of addiction or vice.
- Therapies to prevent suicides.
- Courses or seminars on meditation, yoga, mindfulness.

Treating these problems will help the student's academic performance and personal improvement.

On legislation issues

Each country will be sovereign to create or modify its own laws. But if it seems convenient to accept the resolutions of UELA and adapt them to its legislation. There will be no type of Parliament that legislates on behalf of all member countries.

Latin American Supreme Court of Justice

It will have two chambers. The first will be a Court to see cases of corruption, high treason and attacks against state security by politicians and the military. There will be no appeal. Both for political trials and for court-martials, if found guilty, the accused must be subjected to the maximum penalty.

The second chamber will be the arbitration chamber to see conflicts between UELA countries.

The embassies and diplomatic facilities of UELA both within the member countries and also of its diplomatic corps accredited in the foreign service

The embassies or consulates members of UELA could be gathered in a common building that houses them. Both within member countries and outside them.

Example: the administrative decentralisation building. Architecture: Esteban Bondone, bbgooo associated architects.

Regarding foreign religions brought by European invaders

Although the new Latin American project seeks to eradicate magical and superstitious beliefs in the context of religious customs in the peoples of Latin America, it does not mean that we will be disrespectful to other countries that have an official religion or that have a wide range of beliefs according to their multiculturalism. We wish to have diplomatic relations with all possible States but respect must be reciprocal.

All religious institutions or hierarchies, assemblies to worship divine beings, openly confessing any religious confession will be prohibited.

All practice of sorcery, magic, divination, sorcery, witchcraft, esotericism will be prohibited with severe punishments for those who practice them.

The practice of Freemasonry and all congregation of lodges will be prohibited.

All types of congregation in which idolatry or worship of divine beings is practiced, esoteric or fetishist rituals are performed and superstitious prophecies are propagated will be prohibited.

Religious groups always start as sectarian, fanatical, extremist or fundamentalist groups. These religious groups are manipulated or influenced by leaders or teachers who claim to carry out a messianic salvific mission and are clothed with a certain aura of irrefutable and infallible.

The objective of this is to seek social unity and not be divided by beliefs that throughout history have brought irreparable wars and hatreds.

What will be allowed is that whoever believes in something superior, does so on a personal and individual basis within their home. But, outside of it, they will not be able to openly confess that they are prone to any belief or religious doctrine, nor will they be able to propagate, disseminate or preach their beliefs to other people in order to gain adherents or converts.

What is sought in the citizens of the Latin American Union is that they have broader and more comprehensive thoughts, with a critical sense, and not dogmatic thoughts imposed by a hierarchy through fear of perpetual condemnation in the hereafter.

Only indigenous peoples will be able to practice their beliefs, rites and traditions within their communities.

"Priests do not create, but they do install the religion of fear. Their method is to form a caste that claims to be a mediator between the people and the entities (gods) that they fear. After the caste is established, they begin to exercise their power."

Albert Einstein, German-American physicist

My final reflection on the creation and development of UELA

My fear in the first instance about an international creation of Latin American countries in order to create a regional organisation called UELA is that, in the long run, it will become a circle of bureaucrats who only seek privileges, prestige and status, who are only for what suits them and not for attending to the matters for which the organisation was created, where there is only a bid to preserve particular interests and that year after year they seek to shield themselves with immunity, or that it ends up carrying an agenda only to serve the interests of foreign powers.

STUDY GUIDE

This work is a philosophical-political essay that presents a proposal for the creation of a Union of Latin American States (ULAS), inspired by Simón Bolívar's integrationist ideal. The author, philosopher Jesús Campos, explores the history of Latin America, highlighting the influences of foreign powers such as the British Empire and the United States, and analysing the challenges the region faces in terms of economic development, security, culture and international relations. According to Campos, ULAS would be a response to these challenges, offering a path towards independence, unity and prosperity for Latin American countries.

Challenges and obstacles for ULAS: An in-depth look

The proposal for the Union of Latin American States (ULAS) faces several challenges and obstacles in achieving unity and independence in Latin America:

- Power of vested interests: One of the greatest obstacles lies in the economic elites who benefit from the current system and their relationship with global powers. These elites might oppose ULAS if they perceive it as a threat to their position.

- Ideological dependence: Latin America's dependence on capitalism and communism represents a challenge to autonomy. Breaking away from these models requires a radical shift in socio-economic thinking.

- Foreign influence: The historical influence of foreign powers, especially the United States and the United Kingdom, has left a profound mark on the region. Countering this influence and achieving true independence requires a firm stance.

- Corruption and organised crime: Government corruption and the power of organised crime are obstacles to unity and progress. Combating these issues is crucial for building a solid ULAS.

- Internal differences: Despite similarities, there are historical, political and economic differences among Latin American countries. Overcoming these differences and finding common ground is essential for unity.

- Risk of bureaucratisation: There is a risk that ULAS could become a bureaucratic structure more concerned with its own interests and influence peddling than with the well-being of the region. Establishing mechanisms for transparency and accountability is fundamental.

Overcoming these challenges is essential for ULAS to consolidate itself as a viable and transformative project for Latin America.

How does philosopher Campos propose that ULAS should relate to foreign powers?

ULAS relations with foreign powers: Diplomacy for a new independence.

The philosopher proposes that ULAS should handle foreign powers with caution, seeking real independence and avoiding falling under the influence or control of any nation. The key points of this stance are detailed below:

Active neutrality and non-alignment:

- ULAS declares itself as a non-aligned organisation, meaning it will not position itself as an ally or enemy of any foreign power.

- It seeks to avoid being used as a pawn on the global geopolitical chessboard, rejecting the logic of blocs and alliances that respond to interests foreign to the region.

- This stance implies not being the "backyard" of any power, defending autonomy and sovereign decision-making based on Latin American interests.

Treaties of neutrality and non-intervention:

- The signing of neutrality treaties with powers traditionally influential in the region, such as the United States and the United Kingdom, is proposed.

- These treaties must guarantee non-intervention in the internal affairs of ULAS countries, respecting the sovereignty and self-determination of the region.

- It seeks to end the historical interference of these powers in Latin America, avoiding the repetition of episodes of political or military interventionism.

Demilitarization and end of foreign military presence:

- ULAS will advocate for the demilitarization of Latin American territories occupied by foreign powers, such as Guantanamo in Cuba and the Falkland Islands.

- The withdrawal of foreign military bases in the region will be sought, considering that they violate the sovereignty of countries and fuel unnecessary geopolitical tensions.

- The goal is to make Latin America a zone of peace, free from the military presence of powers foreign to the region.

Conditional cooperation and mutual benefit:

- The possibility of establishing cooperation agreements with other nations is raised, provided they are based on mutual respect, reciprocity and common benefit.

- Priority will be given to cooperation with countries that do not pose a threat to ULAS and that share the values of peace, sustainable development and social justice.

- Dependence on any foreign power will be avoided, seeking self-sufficiency in strategic areas such as the economy, technology and defence.

Firmness in the face of sanctions and threats:

- ULAS will stand firm against any attempt at pressure or sanctions by foreign powers, defending its right to make sovereign decisions.

- Solidarity and mutual support will be sought among the countries of the region to face external pressures and defend common interests.

- Dialogue and diplomacy will be promoted as a means of conflict resolution, but without renouncing the principles of independence and self-determination.

In summary, the philosopher envisions a ULAS that relates to foreign powers from a position of independence and dignity, seeking cooperation on equal terms and firmly defending the autonomy of Latin America.

GLOSSARY OF KEY TERMS:

- ULAS: Union of Latin American States, the regional integration project proposed by the author.
- Hegemony: Predominant dominance or influence of one country or group of countries over others.
- Imperialism: Policy of territorial, economic and cultural expansion and domination of one state over another.
- NATO: North Atlantic Treaty Organisation, a military alliance led by the United States.
- Neoliberalism: Economic doctrine that promotes the reduction of the state's role in the economy.
- Third World: Term used to refer to countries with low socio-economic development.
- Monroe Doctrine: US foreign policy that opposes European intervention in America.
- Holy Alliance: Coalition of European monarchies formed in the 19th century.
- Bretton Woods: Economic agreements signed in 1944 that established the current world financial order.
- World Bank: International financial institution that provides loans to developing countries.
- IMF: International Monetary Fund, a financial organisation that seeks global economic stability.

CONTENT

Jesús Campos was born on December 19, 1969 in Panama City. Son of Jesús Campos and Lilia Vergara, he is the third of five siblings. From a very early age, he felt, like any other child, the fascination of being able to ask questions about everything around him, and the enthusiasm to find the answers to so many questions himself. After completing his secondary studies, he obtained a scholarship to study at the Naval School of Santo Domingo, Dominican Republic. Therefore, he decided to take philosophy as a self-taught vocation. At 18, he continued to ask himself questions, looking for a way to fill and satisfy his deepest and most existential inquiries, to the point that he began to write small sketches and take notes on his readings. He has already published three philosophical essays: *La nueva democracia,* Panama, 2005, an essay on political philosophy; *Introduction to the Study of Human Nature*, Panama, 2020, an essay on anthropological philosophy; and *The Final Decline of the Idols*, Panama, 2021, a philosophical essay on cultural anthropology on religious beliefs and the supernatural. He has also written some articles for local newspapers on literary criticism. In Panama, he has belonged to several literary groups, such as the circle of writers Letras de Fuego (2005), and reading circles such as Guillermo Andreve (2006). On this occasion he launches his most recent essay, entitled *The Americaida*. It is an essay on political philosophy in the geopolitical context of the current situation of the Ibero-American countries that proposes to make an attempt at total integration, similar to the project of the European Union: the Union of Latin American States, UELA. Their political, economic and social realities are almost similar, so a union to solve common problems would be a solution. Two of the major problems to be resolved would be the leap to a robust economic community and being free from the hegemonic interference of any world power.

PRIMERA EDICIÓN
En la composición de este libro
se usó la fuente tipográfica
Helvetica.

Se imprime a partir del mes de
octubre de 2024
por el servicio de impresión
por demanda de Amazon KDP

www.ingramcontent.com/pod-product-compliance
Lightning Source LLC
LaVergne TN
LVHW012110160826
845678LV00014B/3011

9789801854111